A LEAP IN THE DARK

A LEAP IN THE DARK

A Welsh Airman's Adventures in Occupied Europe

by

James Arthur Davies

LEO COOPER
London

First published in Great Britain in 1994 by
LEO COOPER
190 Shaftesbury Avenue, London, WC2H 8JL
an imprint of
Pen & Sword Books Ltd,
47 Church Street, Barnsley, South Yorkshire S70 2AS

Copyright © J. A. Davies, 1994

A CIP catalogue record for this book is available from the British Library

ISBN 0 85052 314 1

Typeset by CentraCet Limited, Cambridge
in 11 point Linotron Garamond

Printed by
Redwood Books,
Trowbridge, Wilts

CONTENTS

Prologue   1

1. Special Duties   15
2. On Our Way   23
3. Friesland   43
4. Five Long Months in Garijp   54
5. South to Brabant   78
6. Belgium   96
7. Behind Bars   100
8. From Brussels to Bankau   108
9. Stalag Luft 7   113
10. The Forced March   140
11. Stalag 3A: Luckenwalde and the Long Liberation   148

Postscript   162

ACKNOWLEDGEMENTS

It would be quite impractical to list the many friends, in war and peace, who have assisted so generously in the preparation of this Memoir. Numerous letters and frequent visits from friends in Holland and Belgium supplemented my own notes which were discovered by my wife, Nesta, during the painful process of moving house.

An airman, shot down on his second raid, and only on an operational Squadron for a few weeks, is hardly the best person to elaborate on his role as a Special Duty Operator, or on life on the Squadron, but my good friend, Ron Hurst, (Herky in the Memoir), possibly the only other survivor from our Special Unit, agreed to 'set the scene', on the clear understanding that I fulfilled my promise to my Dutch friends, and added a 'beginning' as well as an 'end'. I capitulated, and I am most grateful to Ronald Hurst for the Prologue.

My sincere thanks for the observations made by Mrs Tiesinga, Elizabeth Dijkstra, Ruurd Postma, Jaap Boorsma, and Tiny Mulder, on the period in Friesland; the late Simon De Cock, Dina De Cock and Mieke Seys-De Cock on the brief stay in Brabant, and to the guide and courier, Piet Felix who helped me to cross the border into Belgium. Mrs Lucy Leuyten-Staquet introduced me to members of the Witte Brigade, the Belgian Resistance, and enlightened me on the part played by her father in the struggle.

I discussed the prisoner of war camps in Bankau, and later in Luckenwolde, with fellow 'kriegies' Phil Potts, Emrys Williams, Noel Morris, Bill Wiliams and Doug Scourfield, who helped to shed a clearer light on this period.

I am grateful to Miss Iris Challoner, who typed a great deal of the original script and who made critical comments on the 'style'.

My good friend, Richard Gough, not only gave encouragement, but invaluable advice on the presentation, and on the selection of the photographs.

My thanks to the former Archdruid of Wales, James Nicholas, for the 'Englyn', a single-stanza poem, a Welsh metrical form, dating from at least the ninth century. It has been compared with the Greek epigram. He is not responsible for the translation.

Finally my thanks to Nesta, who corrected the many errors in the draft manuscript and in additon became actively involved in the tedious proof-reading process.

Diolch o galon
Heartfelt thanks to you all.

North Sea

Rinsumageest • • Dokkum
Leeuwarden • Garijp Tolbert • Groningen
Eernewoude • • Leek
Grouw • • Oudega • Vries
• Drachten
F R I E S L A N D
Oosterwolde

IJsselmeer

• Kampen

Amsterdam •

H O L L A N D

• The Hague • Utrecht

Neder Rijn • Arnhem
Rotterdam •
Waal
Maas • Nijmegen
• Waalwijk
Kaatsheuvel • • Tilburg

Zundert • Eindhoven

G E R M A N Y
Rhine

Antwerp •

B E L G I U M

• Brussels
Cologne •

• Aachen
Bonn •
Miles
0 10 20 30
Liège •

ENGLYN

An 'Englyn', the oldest recorded Welsh metrical form, dates from at least the ninth century. The Englyn can occur as a single-stanza poem, for which reason it has been compared with the Greek epigram.

Gwelodd wyneb y gelyn – a gwelodd
Wedd ddigalon cyd-ddyn;
Ac yno gweled wedyn
Y mannau da sydd mewn dyn,

He saw the face of the enemy –
He saw despair in his fellow man;
And then he saw the goodness in mankind.

James Nicholas
Welsh poet and Archdruid.
1993.

PROLOGUE

At the end of January, 1944, at the peak of the onslaught by Bomber Command which killed some 600,000 people in Germany and 55,573 British and Commonwealth aircrew, I was one of seven young sergeants deposited from a truck outside the guardroom of a black snowbound airfield in Lincolnshire. A cheerful corporal directed us to dump our kitbags within an equally bleak Nissen hut and ticked our names off his list: Bull, Bryan – who came from Lima, wore appropriate shoulder flashes and was therefore called by us 'Peru' – Davies, Dockerty, Fergus, Herscovitch, who became 'Herky' to the Squadron, and Neille.

That first day Neille left us and sickness took Fergus. Within a few weeks both Bull and Bryan were dead, Bull shot down over Stuttgart and Bryan killed with his crew in attempting an emergency landing at Woodbridge in Suffolk on their return from Frankfurt. As for myself, Sergeant James Arthur Davies, aged 20, I had baled out of a burning Lancaster to become a hunted fugitive in Occupied Europe.

Dockerty, he of the broken nose and dour Yorkshire humour, survived his tour of operations, as did Herky, but remains untraced. It is Herky, therefore, who describes the setting for that strange journey of mine which began at Ludford Magna. His longer experience of life on 101 Squadron and of what we were trained to do there remains clear, whereas the later impressions of my own war do much to obscure that period. Herky now takes up the tale.

J. A. Davies

On that winter morning we knew nothing, save that we had been prematurely plucked from an Operational Training Unit at Hixon, in Staffordshire, designated as 'Special Operators' without regard for painfully acquired aircrew skills and despatched, apprehensive but unresisting and literally at the jerk of a Flight Commander's thumb, to the base of 101 Squadron at Ludford Magna, for Special Duties. Secrecy concealed our future role, but these were the pioneering days of airborne radio countermeasures and the Lancasters of 101 Squadron were dedicated to that operation within the intelligence war that we later learned to call ABC, or Airborne Cigar. Because each of us had owned to a knowledge of German, we had been selected as Special Duty Operators, but at that point told no more: in fact each Special would fly as an extra crew member in aircraft fitted with ABC transmitter/receivers and would have the task of jamming the enemy's night-fighter communications.

This was remote flat farmland, half-way between the whitened country towns of Louth and Market Rasen, with the spires of Lincoln Cathedral thrusting through the mist in the south-west. The Nissen hut in which we now sat, a shelter of windowless corrugated sheets, became home: a rusting stove squatting in the middle of the floorspace, two rows of iron beds, each with its battered wooden locker, and all on a scarred floor of regulation brown linoleum. Hut 8, RAF Ludford Magna, No. 1 Group, Bomber Command.

Across the road from the living area was the airfield. Buried under the drifts were the runways, the perimeter track and the silent aircraft standing on snow-piled, oil-stained dispersals. From the hut it was possible to see the swarm of tiny figures about the Lancasters, clearing fuselages, wings and engines: officers, NCOs and men all shovelling furiously. It was a message we could not fail to understand and it had its response on that first day.

Within a short walk of the airfield's northern perimeter, and dominated by the airfield water-tower, was the village. A single street, a straggle of houses lining the road, the rectory, the school, the two shops of the grocer and the butcher: two inns, the Black Horse and the White Hart and a graceful, ancient church, toylike, at the crest of a gentle, grassy rise and flanked by listing, moss-faced tombstones.

We were summoned to the Specials' Section for an introductory talk by a gaunt Canadian, Flight Lieutenant Bernard Wilkesman. Wilkie is saluted here as a kind and approachable man who cared for those in his charge. He had carried out the first proving flights for the Cigar equipment off the South-Western approaches and then on a survey over Hanover in 1943, to test the receiver and the feasibility of logging enemy transmissions. (A second ABC aircraft was shot down on the return journey.) As a result of those flights and the spadework of a radar expert seconded from Bomber Command, Flight Lieutenant Collins, who oversaw the installation of the equipment and the training of its first batch of Specials, Airborne Cigar became operational in October, 1943. The Lancasters of 101 preceded a similar ABC operation conducted by 214 (Fortress) Squadron, located in Norfolk, again organized by Collins, under the aegis of 100 (Special Duties) Group, Bomber Command. (The first man to greet me at Ludford was a Special, Sergeant Lander, who told me he was to join 214 Squadron.)

Wilkie had recently taken over the Special Section from Flight Lieutenant Duringer who had been lost at the beginning of January while on his second tour of operations. We sat before Wilkie as he outlined our duties and the nature of the German night-fighter communications system which we were to penetrate. Detailed studies of these control systems now exist in excellent works such as Alfred Price's *Instruments of Darkness*, R. V. Jones's *Most Secret War* and Martin Streetly's *Confound and Destroy*: all are the stuff of experience and scholarly peacetime research, but at that point, early in 1944, we were still struggling to gain and make use of information from sources implacably closed to us. The tools for this were the ground and airborne equipment provided by our own Telecommunications Research Establishment (TRE), at Malvern, under Dr (later, Sir) Robert Cockburn, amplified by continuing analysis of what could be gleaned on each flight.

It suffices here that we learned that the enemy defence was based on a series of geographic 'boxes' – the *Himmelbet* or 'Heavenly Bed' system originated by General Kammhuber (by then ignominiously dismissed by Hitler for the shortcomings of the air defences; although Kammhuber was more fortunate than the Luftwaffe's General Jeschonnek who committed suicide one month later).

Within the boxes, the urgently scrambled fighters orbited about a radio beacon and were directed by controllers on to headings which would intercept the bombers. This was the *Zahme Sau* or Tame Boar technique. Kammhuber's successor, Hajo Herman, added a refinement known as *Wilde Sau* or Wild Boar which relied on visual instead of radar interception and was thus less vulnerable to our attentions: but the general dependence on spoken instructions, whether for individual guidance or in 'running commentaries' by the German controllers, left the fighter pilots and their controllers open to the harassment of jamming by the Specials. What we were unsure of at that time, among so many other preoccupations, was the extent to which any signals we transmitted might serve as homing beacons for the fighters.

In the hut, later that day, Neille told us that he would have nothing to do with this business. He stood his ground through what we guessed was a very stormy interview with the Commanding Officer and then disappeared from our lives, not even being permitted to return to the hut for his kit lest he infect us with similar ideas. Rumour had it that he was spirited away to Burma: if that was true, it would have been a sensible attempt to protect the embarrassing information he had been so trustingly given.

That evening Fergus became obviously ill and was borne away by medical orderlies.

Sombre, perplexed and now five, we sought relief in the Sergeants' Mess, a larger version of Hut 8 but with a lounge and a bar and dozens of spartan, worn armchairs in which sprawled a noisy clientele, a kaleidoscope of navy and Air Force blue uniforms: Australians, New Zealanders, Canadians, South African, Rhodesian and British aircrew, all of them very much at home. They catcalled, argued or talked earnestly while some joined the phalanx beating at the still-shuttered bar with a steady chant of 'Open up, open up'. It became a roar of triumph as the blind rolled obligingly upward and a mess corporal prepared to field the orders. It seemed that chaos reigned, but we noted that every man who entered the Mess had made a beeline for the noticeboard opposite the doorway. We ourselves had not yet seen a Battle Order, but it would be the appearance of one of those direful typewritten sheets, in due time bearing our own names, which would likewise turn us into compulsive readers.

We ate the evening meal, returned to the lounge and, suiting our raw status, made our own laager in a corner. Our seniors and therefore betters involved themselves in ad hoc rugby games, raucous horseplay and determined drinking contests with yards of ale, and since there were five of us to share the journey to the bar we became slowly forgetful of the day. In this we were nobly aided by Peru, who told us what we thought were scandalous stories of Lima, drew us into laughter and, soon, into clowning. Snapping his fingers, red forelock falling over blissfully rolling eyes, he came to his feet and began to sing. We formed a line behind him, joined soon by others: a happy, hilarious snake reeling around the room in a mad figure-of-eight conga, everyone clumsy with the lovely new words:

> *La Cucaraca*
> *la Cucaraca*
> *ya no puede caminar . . .*
> *porque no tiene*
> *porque le falta*
> *mariguana pa fumar.*

It became our song.

In the Special Section's workshop the next day we were shown the equipment we would use. This was a compact grouping of units: the ABC receiver with a cathode ray tube and three jamming transmitters, designed to cover the fighter control frequencies of 38.3–42.5 Mc/s. Our NCO instructor set up a signal generator to simulate the German transmissions, plugged in our headsets and pointed to the CRT screen on which a bright green base line now appeared. On the line, minute pulses shimmered and as the 'controller' spoke, a taller pulse sprang into view, abruptly disappearing as the 'message' ended.

The skill to be practised lay in quickly tuning the receiver to the German signal, first to listen and then to log anything of importance. This included such phenomena as enemy call-signs, changes of control methods, ie, from male to female speakers, use of music or Morse as coded signals, switching of frequencies to evade our countermeasures, exact time for purposes of location, size of 'blip' and strength of signal. We were then to overlay the signal with the jammer which produced a warbling note blanketing the enemy transmission, and continue to investigate new signals until each of our three jammers was in action. With experience came cunning on both sides and, in our case, the ability to deal with new ploys adopted by the enemy, such as decoy signals.

Our work in flight was monitored by the ground section at Kingsdown, near Canterbury. This was a major centre of the countermeasures war, from where jamming and verbal transmissions disrupted the night-fighter control system, the voices being provided by German-speaking Special Operators as well as by gramophone recordings. As was the case in the Special Section at Ludford, many of the operators were Jewish refugees from Nazi Germany. The added risks and terrors for such people on flying operations over their late homeland can be imagined; their courage cannot.

In addition to making life difficult for enemy controllers and pilots in this way, the information was clearly vital to the planning of future raids. Our logs would therefore be collected by our Section Leader at our own debriefing, or by his deputy, Flight Lieutenant G. D. Smith if Wilkie was flying, and would immediately be sent off to some unexplained destination for evaluation before the next operation. These facts being plain, we applied ourselves to our lessons and took in whatever more experienced Specials could tell us. We also learned something of the anatomy of our equipment from the Workshop NCOs, Sergeant Foster and Corporal Mustoe.

We were, of course, ordered never to discuss our work with anyone else, not even with our tantalised crews who suspected much but were not in the secret: but the ABC aircraft carried two massive dorsal aerials with a third offset vertically at the nose. Given that eccentricity and the rare sight of the Special hunched over a glowing screen in the darkness of his isolated midships position – isolated, too, for much of the flight from the crew intercom – the guesswork was inevitable, but remained unsatisfied. In fact, apart from those connected with the Section, only two, or at most three, of the Station's senior officers – the base Commander, Air Commodore Blucke, Group Captain Patrick King, the Station Commander and (possibly) Wing Commander Alexander, the Squadron Commander – had any clear idea of the ABC operation. There may have been two people at Group Headquarters for necessary liaison with the Section and certainly very few at Bomber Command Head-quarters at High Wycombe.

The enigma of the ABC operation for those outside the Special Duties Section is summed up in a letter contributed to the RAF Amateur Radio Society in Spring, 1992, by one of 101's radar mechanics, Gerry Parfitt:

'The ABC equipment literally did "appear". One would go out on a Daily Inspection (of the aircraft) one morning to find racking where there had been nothing the day before. Later, mysterious equipment would be fitted there, with an obvious radio background and a cathode ray tube. Being a radar mechanic, the only trade to have CRT's, I knew it wasn't ours and nobody else knew what it was – or said they didn't.'

But for Gerry Parfitt, and doubtless for others, there were clues: '101 Squadron was the only one to have eight crew members and it was only on seeing that the name of the eighth member was (frequently) of Germanic or European origin that one realized the purpose of this equipment.'

Between 4 and 8 February we put in three brief cross-country flights in order to familiarize ourselves with the Squadron aircraft. These flights in bright daylight were not yet the serious expeditions soon to come and after we had checked out the layout of the ABC station, the positions of the portable oxygen bottle and the sockets for the main supply and the intercom, it was pleasant to be virtually an idle passenger. Standing by the pilot, it was possible to pick out the airfields crawling below us at around 160 m.p.h: our neighbouring field, Binbrook, then the runways of Hemswell, Faldingworth, Wickenby, Dunholm Lodge . . . a dip of the wing about Lincoln, a view of The Wash: along the coast to Mablethorpe, to Spurn Head and Grimsby: and then the leisurely 180 degrees turn to approach Ludford.

In our free time, away from the Section, we acquired bicycles, a thriving market being sustained by 101's transient owner-ship, chose Ludford's Black Horse as our own local, disdaining the White Hart faction, and explored the vicinity. From the roadside we could always find a lift to Louth or Lincoln: more pubs, of course – save for cinemas, or possibly a dance, and a meal, there was nowhere else to go – and one thoughtful walk, to the nearby village of Tealby. Two amiable ladies there, the Misses Howell, kept a tea garden: they peered at Peru's exotic shoulder flash and wished to know what part of Canada was that.

And on Tuesday, 15 February we went to the Mess for breakfast and afterwards saw our names on the Battle Order, serial number 466, for that night's operation.

The Squadron was to supply 23 aircraft and all five new Specials were to fly: Dockerty with Flight Sergeant Bateman, RCAF, Bryant with Flight Sergeant Carson, RCAF, Bull with Flight Sergeant Clegg, Herky with Flight Sergeant Kidd and Davies with the South African, Warrant Officer Laurens. (Later Kidd and his crew went to a Pathfinder Squadron: Lewis (Chuck) Bateman and Matthew (Kit) Carson were commissioned and carried two extremely fortunate Specials,

Dockerty and Herky, safely, although not uneventfully, through the remainder of their tour.)

The inescapable Tannoy called us to the guarded, window-shrouded Operations Room for briefing. Seated in rows before the curtained map on the end wall, something like two hundred aircrew packed the room. One character occasioned some local merriment and much craning of necks with an imaginative addition to his battledress – an opera cloak and top hat.

Cigarette smoke rose over muttered conversation which stilled with the arrival of the Station Commander and his retinue. We shuffled clumsily to our feet, were waved down and watched as the curtain was drawn aside to reveal the huge map of Occupied Europe and our first intimation of that night's target.

A crimson ribbon pinned to the map at Ludford Magna ran eastward to a point off Esbjerg and from there darted southwest to Berlin. The return leg skirted the Ruhr but gave a straight run across Holland for base.

The sudden murmur from the crews was the spoken dismay of many who had been raiding the Big City since November, 1943, and who knew only too well the cost of the Battle of Berlin. History notes that this was to be the end of that battle, that 891 aircraft were engaged that night and that 43 aircraft would fail to return: but at that moment this was but another operation to endure. The room relapsed into silence as the ritual of briefing went on and the Squadron Commander's survey of the proposed operation was supported in turn by information from the Navigation, Bombing, Signals and Engineering Leaders. It was forcefed, and vital that it be understood. We paid attention, therefore, to the arcana of the target marking systems.

The penultimate lecturer – for the Squadron Commander would close the briefing by wishing us luck – was the unfortunate Met Officer; without the plethora of global information available today and, indeed, it seemed to us, little more knowledge than could be gained from simply looking out of the window, his forecasts were greeted with unconcealed scepticism. Veterans had found that Met promises of ten-tenths cloud over the target had too often been realized, not there, but over Ludford Magna on return.

An hour before take-off the crews boarded trucks amid much black buffoonery of scuffling and were dropped off at their respective aircraft to make final checks at their stations and to await the order to start engines. Behind us lay the 'ops meal' with its privileged egg, and some stressful, hard-to-kill hours in the hut during which people smoked, read magazines, talked or wrote letters, the while keeping private fears to themselves. Jim Davies wrote to his parents:

'. . . the letter was charged with emotion and makes embarrassing reading today for it was a letter of apology. I gave it to my friend Herky who promised to post it if I did not return. It was given to me many years later in an envelope marked "Strictly Confidential" . . .'

In the parachute and dressing rooms we had collected flying suits, fur-lined boots, an electrical overall with contacts for wired gloves and inner slippers, silk inner gloves, gauntlets, Mae Wests, oxygen masks and helmets. We put on the parachute harness and gingerly carried our parachute packs, taking great care not to pick them up inadvertently by the rip-cord handle. Tucked into our inner clothing was the 'escape pack', of which more will be said. The Duty crew had already provisioned the aircraft with packed sandwiches and thermos flasks of coffee and with rations of sweets which left mouths sickly with glucose under our masks.

Our checks completed, there was nothing now but that wait. For a little time we could sit outside the aircraft, fool about and smoke. We saw a tiny car stop at each dispersal: soon it came to us, bringing the Commanding Officer and a desperately embarrassed Chaplain for a final word of encouragement. And at long last we climbed aboard again to settle into our seats, to watch for the first propeller blades to begin their slow rotation and to hear the first chugging cough become a roar, the blades blur and the noise taken up and enhanced in turn by every Lancaster on the field.

Heavy with bombs and fuel-load, we joined the procession of aircraft waddling from the dispersals to the runway. We passed as we went an audience of WAAFs, officers and airmen who waved solemnly as we trundled onward.

Flight Sergeant Kidd aligned the aircraft at the end of the runway, called the crew to readiness and, as the Aldis winked green from the caravan at precisely 1745 hours, lifted Lancaster SR N-Nan, into the air.

In the night about N-Nan hundreds of aircraft climbed on track, outward across the North Sea.

Masked and goggled the Specials sat huddled in their own darkness. For a short spell they could take comfort from the calm voices of their crews, but as the bomber stream approached the coast of Denmark it was time to shut off the intercom and switch on the ABC.

The cathode screen came slowly to life. Soon the first murmurings were heard in the earphones, the bright trace appeared on the screen and on the trace the first, faint signs of activity. Pulses leapt into view. Like the voices, they grew in clarity as the bomber went deeper into enemy airspace, until, in the region of the fighter beacons and in the target area, the speakers and their mood could be clearly identified – urgent, assured, chillingly triumphant and congratulatory: male voices, female voices: all interspersed by the demented warbling of the jammers. Gloved hands scribbled in logs and fraying electric gloves enlived the dark with sparks as they touched the ABC switches.

At twenty thousand feet intense cold gripped the men at the unheated Special stations. The metal walls of the fuselage were coated in a rime of frost and from time to time it was necessary for the Special to free the oxygen mask from ice. Electric suits warded off actual hypothermia, but their performance was unpredictable. Many Specials, finding that the suits produced near-volcanic temperatures and trouser legs charred to powder, periodically unplugged them from the electrical supply during the flight. To the ambience of near-complete darkness, isolation and tension was thus added the traumatic effects of repeated changes of temperature from one extreme to the other over a period of some hours: and this in an unpressurized aircraft with an established noise level of 120 decibels at the Special's station. It is no surprise that postwar deafness became a common legacy.

In these conditions and at 2130 hours the bombers turned on to their final, southerly heading for the target. North of the city fighter flares illuminated a reddened sky; above the aiming points brilliant red and green target indicators drifted slowly down. A heavy barrage of flak filled the air with flashes and black smoke and, among this turmoil, searchlights groped, coned luckless aircraft and held them, pinned for the guns. Stricken bombers fell engulfed in fire and in such numbers that it was thought necessary to lie to the aircrews of Bomber Command to prevent their demoralization. Many of those ghastly eruptions, they were told, were merely giant fireworks, called Scarecrows; it was assumed that we would feel better if we attributed to other causes the Bomber Command losses announced daily by the BBC and all those mocking empty beds in the Nissen huts.

Decades later, research by the authors Len Deighton (*Bomber*, Pan Books, London, 1970) and Max Hastings (*Bomber Command*, Michael Joseph, London, 1979) confirmed that there were no such devices as Scarecrows in the German armoury and that what the aircrews saw was indeed the immolation of their friends.

The Specials, of course, from their windowless midships position, could not normally witness these fearful scenes: but their station lay on the port side of the bomb-bay and if a bomb-bay inspection slot was removed while the bay was open over the target, the whole terrible panorama of flame and smoke was revealed below. The very air reeked: scatters of burning incendiaries glowed as far as could be seen and every few seconds came new explosions on the ground and the thump of shockwaves against hull and wings.

It was not possible to look for long: kneeling beside the open bay, a rushing slipstream tore through the aperture. The wind would force the viewers' goggles upward like spectacles pushed to the brow and the exposed eyes would immediately fill with freezing tears.

Furtive, hunted, its crew tired and animal-alert, N-Nan fled west, slinking across Germany, the Netherlands, the sea, to glimpse at last the coast of Britain and soon, the blessed, occulting Morse of Ludford's beacon. Wary now of other black shapes in the circuit, N-Nan announced her arrival, found the funnel in her turn, touched down, slowed and began to taxi back to her dispersal. Long free of his duties, the Special gathered parachute pack and ABC log, made his unsteady way aft and opened the rear door. A few minutes after midnight, after seven hours aloft, he stood watching the beautiful English tarmac rolling by.

Of the 43 aircraft and 324 men brought down that night by the fighters, flak, collision or unexplained mishap, one Lancaster, SR-G-George, belonged to 101 Squadron. This was P/O McConnell's crew: we had encountered the Special, P/O Fischl, in the Section and regarded him as a veteran. It was another revelation that operational experience conferred no immunity.

In this manner were the new Specials initiated into their trade.

Four days later, on Saturday, 19 February, we flew to Leipzig and Jack Laurens' K-King failed to return. When it was clear that the aircraft was overdue beyond hope and that nothing had been heard of her since take-off, I left the Operations Room, went back to Hut 8 and told the others.

The next day I posted Jim Davies' letter to his parents in Wales and watched as two Police Corporals packed his kit. We were not left long to brood. The rumour of ops, electrifying the Station and cutting off all communication with the world outside, was confirmed on the Mess notice-board. Our names were among the twenty-two crews on Battle Order 471 for Sunday, 20 February.

And at 2345 hours that night we took off again, myself in N-Nan, for Stuttgart.

CHAPTER ONE

SPECIAL DUTIES

Herky, the incredibly lucky survivor, was admirably qualified to set the scene at Ludford, this wartime airfield embedded in winter mud which we immediately christened Mudford. We were both convinced that after these few cross-country flights we would be sent home for a long leave before becoming operational. I was so confident that I wrote to my parents to tell them that I had been recommended for a commission and that I would be with them within a few days to tell them all about my new duties. An empty promise. Hopes unfulfilled. We were both to be operational within hours. We were stunned by this unexpected directive and could not understand why our promised leave had been cancelled.

Before we arrived at the squadron we were vaguely aware of the risks and knew that there would be casualties, but we believed that this only happened to others. Others were killed, other were wounded, others were taken prisoner. However, the concealed tension in our billet and three empty beds were a constant reminder that the others could easily be us. Max Hastings quotes in *Bomber Command* the words of Flight-Lieutenant Dennis Hornsey in 1943: 'If you live on the brink of death yourself, it is as if those who have gone have merely caught an earlier train to the same destination, and wherever that destination is, you will be sharing it soon, since you will be almost certainly catching the next one.'

The five of us discussed this new directive and four of us decided that although we were volunteers and were free to refuse, we had no alternative. We were not heroes or as stupid as post-war generations might think. We had all volunteered for

15

air-crew duties and for these Special Duty operations, and had waited a long time for the opportunity to be posted to an operational squadron. We had enjoyed the privileges and prestige of having a wing or half a wing on our tunics and we had our pride. To have refused to go required a kind of courage which I did not possess. Four of us had no doubts and decided that we had to go, though we were probably as scared as Neille, who refused. The great morale-booster in this miserable little nissen hut was Herky who was supremely confident that all would be well.

Little wonder that our leave was cancelled. In 1943 and during the first few months of 1944, Bomber Command was being shot out of the sky by the highly skilled German night-fighter force, now equipped with airborne radar sets code-named 'Leichtenstein'. This new technology enabled the fighter pilots to approach the bombers from a range spanning from three miles to visual distance.

The Canadian lawyer and former Bomber Pilot, D. F. Peden, QC, DFM, enlisted the views of two of our previous 'enemies' as to the effectiveness of our electronic counter-measures, General Adolf Galland, the General Inspector of the German Fighter Army, and General Josef Kammhuber, a former Inspector of the West German Airforce. General Galland, in his book *The First and the Last*, paid special attention to the counter-measures of our Number 100 Group, referring to 'the highly successful operations with its broad spectrum of tactics and techniques'. He concluded his letter to Peden with these words: 'The combination of the Pathfinders' operations, the activities of the 100 Group, the British advantage in radar, jamming and Window techniques combined with intelligent attacking tactics, as well as on the other hand the discipline and bravery of the RAF crews have been remarkable. We had our severe problems in trying to defend Germany in the air.' General Kammhuber was more cautious in his assessment of our role, but had to admit that our 'changing electronic tactics were always setting the Luftwaffe Night Fighter Command new problems to solve'.

In spite of the existing counter-measures, by mid-1943 the

bomber loss rate was approaching the maximum that our lords and masters in High Wycombe considered to be acceptable – 200 four-engined bombers a month. In the Battle of Berlin between November, 1943, and March, 1944, the RAF suffered 1077 bombers lost and 1862 damaged. At this rate Bomber Command would cease to exist. In the offensive in which Herkey took part against the cities of Germany 55,573 aircrew, all officers and non-commissioned officers, were killed and a further 9,784 were shot down and taken prisoner. In the brilliantly researched book *Bomber Command* Max Hastings reminds us that the sacrifice was greater than the British Army's total loss of officers in the First World War. Just a few more statistics as I am anxious to explain, if not to justify, the cancellation of our promised leave. Bomber Command's casualties amounted to almost one-seventh of all British deaths in action. The equivalent of the whole front line Bomber force was wiped out every twenty trips. The average number of operations per aircrew over all Bomber Command was 9.1, and only one third of all bomber aircrew completed a first tour.

I now know why our leave was cancelled; immediate replacements were urgently required and we fulfilled this role. Some of us survived. Recently I came across a book which was published in 1957 called *101 Nights* by Roy Ollis of Port Smith in Kenya. A special security release had enabled him to base the story on the hitherto secret activities of 101 Squadron. He describes the Special Duty Operators as 'Twenty-eight nightingales, not killing enemies but saving airmen's lives'. This makes me feel very virtuous but the nightingale was also a member of a crew of eight on a bombing operation. We flew over the target and we dropped our bombs. Ollis also wrote: 'I've heard that 101 are on some new special duties task. I hope not. Special duties usually means you stick your neck out even further'.

I became the Special Duty Operator in Lancaster K-King 237 and flew with Warrant Officer Jack Laurens, DFM, and his experienced crew, known as the 'League of Nations Crew'. We regarded our Skipper Jack as rather elderly – he was 26 years of age. He was a tall, well-built South African from Cape Town, a strange mixture of a practical joker and a serious thinker. About eighteen months after leaving school he went to England and served with the Grenadier Guards until he was wounded at Dunkirk. He applied for a transfer to the RAF and was trained in Canada. He was the only married member of the crew and had completed eighteen missions over Europe.

The 22-year-old Navigator, Les Burton, came from Calverley in Yorkshire and was one of the original crew members. I met him for the first time since 1945 at a Squadron Reunion in Ludford in 1980 when he gave me a detailed, modest and unemotional summary of his activities in the squadron during the 'Great Battles' of 1943 and 1944. He recalled that between November, 1943, and February, 1944, he had taken part in twelve trips to Berlin in addition to raids on Dusseldorf, the Mont Cenis tunnel in Modane in the Alps, Leipzig, Stettin, Brunswick and Magdeburg. Altogether Les completed over thirty trips over 'Fortress Europe' during a period of intense anti-aircraft activity from the ground and also from the highly effective German 'Wild Boar' night-fighter squadrons. His comment on the Mont Cenis raid was that he was probably the only navigator who didn't know the height of Monc Blanc and went up to 26,000 feet just to make sure. The result was that on the way home K-King had to land at Hurn on the south coast with dry tanks. On the Stettin operation, he was routed over Norway and the raid lasted 9 hours and 15 minutes, with a long sea leg on the final run home. They were caught in a dramatic thunderstorm on the way home from Berlin on 20 January, 1944, with almost two hours of incessant lightning and hail with slabs of ice being thrown from the props against the fuselage. The Flight Engineer had to help Jack to hold the control column steady as the vibration was so intense, with blue lights running round the window frames and jumping across the gun barrels. The following night another Lancaster passed over the top of K-King so close that it removed the aerial mast by the astro dome. The mid-upper turret was smashed by the mast.

Les, like Herky, had witnessed one of the biggest pyrotechnic displays in Europe, but only mentioned the natural hazards of thunderstorms and the risks of colliding with your own bombers over to the target.

Jack had the same crew for all these raids with the exception of the French-Canadian Bomb Aimer, Jacques Marchant, who had a bout of influenza and missed a few trips. By the time he had recovered we had gone missing and he had the choice of flying with a new crew or to return home to Montreal. He went home. He had heard that we had gone down in flames and that we were all dead.

Sergeant Ronald Aitken was Marchant's replacement and had made just one trip with this crew. He came from Oldham but all my attempts to locate him have been in vain. Sergeant William Alex George Kibble, our Flight Engineer, came from Hatfield in Hertfordshire, Sergeant William Frederick Donald Bolt, the Mid-Upper Gunner, from Plymouth, and the Rear Gunner, Sergeant Albert Edward Royston, from Dorfield near Barnsley. The only member of the crew already commissioned was the Radio Operator, Pilot Officer Cassian Henry Waight from Belize in British Honduras. I was the eighth member described in a Dutch book *Gevlengeld Verleden* as a slender and 'intelligence' boy from Wales. The slender boy from Wales had complete confidence in this seasoned and highly efficient crew.

In the chapter on Bomber Command Headquarters, Max Hastings informs us that the Commander-in-Chief, known to us as Butcher Harris, had a working day which ended at the same time as that of any businessman, around 6pm: 'It is one of the ironies of the Bomber Offensive that while aircrew fought through the darkness over Germany, while the sleepless cities stood to their guns and searchlights and burst forth in their nightly torment of fire and blast, the Commander-in-Chief of Bomber Command lay dreamless in his bed among the Buckinghamshire woods.' I don't know whether this is fair comment; possibly the Commander who justified the controversial bombing of the German cities by enlisting the support of the Old Testament prophet, Hosea – 'They have sown the wind and they shall reap the whirlwind' – may have had an occasional sleepless night.

Monday the fourteenth of February, when our names appeared on the Battle Order, was only one of the tortuous days and nights in 1943 and early 1944 when he was able to implement the Biblical threat. The dream of the romantic airman was shattered on this St Valentine's Day in 1944, and though we all put on a splendid act of indifference, the long journey from Ludford to Berlin and back and the ferocious city defences did not make my first operational trip an attractive proposition.

K-King had to carry eight crew members, sophisticated heavy equipment, and in addition an Elsan chemical toilet placed awkwardly at the rear of the fuselage. This brilliant and thoughtful piece of planning was a good morale booster but hardly ever used. Anyone who succeeded in using it in the Battle of Berlin was worthy of any decoration which His Majesty's Government would be prepared to confer. It was a major operation. It meant the plugging-in and the un-plugging of the inter-com and oxygen bottles and crawling in the darkness through the narrow and congested fuselage in a bitterly cold atmosphere at twenty thousand feet. Having succeeded in the immediate objective you removed two pairs of gloves, fumbled with your reinforced underwear, your electrically heated trousers, and eventually returned to your central source of oxygen to do the things you were supposed to do. It would be over seven and a half hours before we returned to base but we did not accept the Elsan challenge. The disciplined crew of K-King emptied their bladders over the bleak Lincolnshire Wolds before taking up their allotted places within the aircraft. I suppose the post-war owner of the airfield knew that the combined efforts of countless crews would contribute significantly to the fertility of the soil. A splendid investment for a shrewd farmer.

I have the greatest difficulty in recalling this Berlin mission. The very last item in my diary reads: 'After a night-out in Louth, the nearest town, we went on Monday to the 'Big City' – Berlin. The weather was not very favourable but we came

1. 1615898 Warrant Officer Davies, J.A.

2. A typical scene at Ludford Magna,
   predictably called Mudford Magna by
   the men of 101 Squadron.

3. Jack Laurens (left) with the crew of Lancaster DV 267 − K King (*see p 13*).

4. A 101 Squadron Lancaster on a bombing run to Berlin. The bombs include the large blockb... and smaller incendiaries. Note the dorsal fin in front of the turret for the airborne cigar jamm... transmitters operated by the Specials. (*Central Office of Information*).

5. Interlude at snowbound Ludford Magna. Herky (*centre: see p 1*) with (*left*) MacLeod and (*right*) Dockerty, 'he of the broken nose and dour Yorkshire humour', February, 1944.

'I was received with great warmth by . . . Den Heer and Mevrouw Tiesinga and later met their three young children' (*p 45*).

7. The author (*right*) at Romsicht Farm, Oosterwolde, February, 1944. Note my companion's clogs.

8. 'An attractive 22-year-old girl called Tiny Mulder' (*p 48*).

9. The Dijkstra family at Garijp — Pieter, Elisabeth and Hinke (*see p 52*).

home without any serious incident, though we nearly collided with another Lanc over the target – unpleasant.'

All appeared to be going according to plan. I was in a little world of my own, stuck in front of my powerful transmitter, and in glorious isolation from the other members of the crew. The blips on my screen were the only reminders that there was intense fighter activity outside. We were now approaching the target. I was listening intently to the German controllers when Jack made a dramatic dive to avoid a head-on collision with another Lancaster. Clearly imprinted on my memory is seeing my thermos flask of hot coffee and the rubber-insulated torch suddenly suspended in mid-air. A few seconds later a shattered thermos flask and a torch observed the laws of gravity. I switched off my German transmitter and for the first time witnessed the action outside. A dull red glow was reflected in the clouds and the normally dark sky was now alight with shells, searchlights and a crippled Lancaster going down in flames.

This brief glimpse made me realize how vulnerable we were. The desperate evasive action was completed and a very level flight over the target followed. Bombs gone, and home to our bacon and eggs.

A few years ago one of the most distinguished war correspondents, Wynford Vaughan Thomas, and I were speaking at the same function. In his opening remarks he said, 'You have with you this evening the only two guest speakers who went once only to Berlin in a Lancaster and came back.'

The weather conditions were absolutely foul over East Anglia during the next few days with the word 'scrubbed', meaning a cancelled operation, acquiring a new meaning, synonymous with frustration or relief depending on the mood you were in. The Tannoy still functioned loud and clear: 'All operational crew report to the Briefing Room.' The same pattern as before – the Station Commander's laudable effort to bolster up morale, bacon and eggs, flying gear, and then just before take-off – 'Scrubbed'. We shuffled back to our billet. Another wasted effort, but another trip to our personal Big City, Louth.

There were good reasons for these last-minute cancelled operations due entirely to the weather, such as fog, icing or high cloud cover. On Saturday, 19 February it had been snowing all day and, quite confident that we would not be ordered to fly, we prepared ourselves for another night of sheer escapism in our adopted market town. The Combined Chiefs of Staff, however, had other ideas, and on 13 February, 1944, ordered an intensive bomber offensive against Germany, the 'Big Week' of air attacks to be from 19 to 26 February. There had been too many delays, the weather was to be ignored, and the red tape on the big map in the Briefing Room stretched as far as Leipzig.

I noticed as we boarded our trucks that Herky had a pair of light civilian shoes slung over his shoulder, and when I asked him the reason for this addition to our standard equipment, his answer was most revealing. These were his last words before we joined our respective crews: 'My friend, if you are shot down you will either be killed or taken to a proper Prison Camp under the control of the Geneva Convention. I am a Jew, and as the Herrenvolk would like to liquidate my race, I aim to get away from the wreckage as soon as possible. How can you possibly do that in heavy, fur-lined flying boots?' Herky had no occasion to use his shoes. He lived on the brink of death, completed 36 raids over Europe and was still at Ludford Magna over a year after we first met.

CHAPTER TWO

ON OUR WAY

The weather was grim with heavy rain and very low cloud, the cloud base being only 2,000 feet when Lancaster D.V 267 – K-King – took off from Ludford Magna at 2338 hours on 19 February, 1944. Target – Leipzig. Twenty-two aircraft from our squadron formed part of a combined force of 844 Lancasters and Halifaxes detailed to take part in this mission.

Our Skipper was instructed not to do the usual circuit around Ludford, but to climb in a northerly direction until we broke cloud, and then to return to the rendezvous position at Mablethorpe on the Lincolnshire coast. This was to reduce the risk of collisions in the clouds whilst climbing. We broke cloud at about 12,000 feet and on our return to Mablethorpe Les, our Navigator, obtained a wind velocity and direction to apply to the next course. This was to a position in the North Sea approximately 54 degrees North and 4.40 degrees East, from which we were to turn on to a South-East course to make landfall between Ameland and the Schiermonnokoog islands at 2.30 in the morning.

Above the North Sea Les discovered that the wind was much stronger than that which was given at the briefing, and as a result of this unexpected tail wind, and to avoid arriving too early at the turning point, a number of dog-legs were carried out. According to the weather forecast, a wind force of about 100 hundred miles an hour was to be expected at a height of 20,000 feet. During the climb, and in the short time we flew over England, the wind was indeed at a speed of 100 miles an hour, but coming from another direction, presenting Les with the problem of which wind he would use in making his calculations and timing. He was a competent Navigator and solved this very minor difficulty.

Five of the crew were in the front of the aircraft and almost within touching distance – the Pilot, Navigator, Flight-Engineer, Bomb-Aimer and Wireless Operator. The Mid-Upper and Rear Gunners were ensconced in their lonely turrets. I was in a cloistered and isolated private little cell concentrating on the almost hypnotic blips on a little screen and tuned in to a German woman controller known to us as 'The Bitch of Bragdenburg'. There was no contact with the other members of the crew. My isolation nearly cost me my life.

Somewhere over German-occupied Friesland the Wireless Operator announced that an interceptor fighter was approaching; this appeared on his screen in the form of a blip on the newly installed radar instrument. Jack was busy preparing to make an escape manoeuvre and as his crew waited tensely for the plane to go into a corkscrew, the Wireless Operator announced almost immediately, 'It's all right, he is going away – 300 yards, 500 yards OK.' Perhaps he had read the information on his set wrongly, or there were other reasons, but it was not all right and not OK. The interceptor had not gone away.

A loud drum-like noise was audible and vicious tongues of flame illuminated the dark and starless sky. Flames poured in from the direction of the port outer engine. This did not cause undue alarm at first as Jack and Alex assumed that it was only one of the port-wing engines which was on fire. This had happened to them on two or three previous occasions and they knew what to do. They put their fire-extinguishers to work, 'feathered' the propeller and the port-wing engine stopped burning. Alex switched all the four engines on to the starboard centre tank in order to use up as much petrol as possible in an attempt to control the flames, but, as they increased in intensity, he realized that the wing tank between both port-side engines had been holed and each tank containing some 400 gallons of high-octane fuel was ablaze. The crippled Lancaster could never reach the target and it was clear that we had to try to return to England.

Les gave Jack a course of 270 degrees due west with the intention of working out the refinements later. "Due west" was good enough at the time. Decisions had to be taken very quickly now as parts of the wing were peeling back and the flames were bursting through the frail skin of the Lanc towards the rear of the plane.

Jack's immediate reaction was to make for the North Sea and get into an inflatable dinghy, but Les convinced him that we would never make it as the wing could never hold for that distance. In any case the prospect of ditching in the icy cold North Sea with a wind of 100 miles an hour at 2.40 in the morning was not an attractive proposition.

After considering the possibility of losing height and crash-landing over land or even landing on a German fighter drome, the only sensible solution seemed to be to bale out while we were still over land and put our faith in our parachutes. The decision had been made.

While all this was taking place, I was still carrying out my 'Nightingale' activities, in touch with the German controllers, but oblivious of the drama which was being enacted within K-King. Then I noticed for the first time the emergency red warning lights on my table. I switched on the inter-com and became aware of the very real, immediate and desperately urgent situation all around me. The crew were already at their 'Prepare to Abandon' positions in the aircraft and were preparing to leave, waiting for the final command. The plane was now burning furiously. There was a sickly smell of cordite.

The two Gunners, Ted Royston and Don Bolt, were unable to open the rear door from which three of us had to jump. Jack Laurens was shouting instructions until the very end: 'Have you jettisoned the bombs yet, Bomb Aimer?' and the very last words I heard were those of the Mid-Upper Gunner saying that the escape door at the rear was jammed and that he could not open it. Jack's final words before giving his last command was to tell my friend in no uncertain terms, and in language worthy of an ex-Grenadier Guardsman, to get the axe and smash it open.

At the same time Ron Aitken was having difficulty in removing the hatch in the nose of the plane, and their means of escape was temporarily blocked. With the help of Alex they eventually released it.

After a few seconds Les grabbed a parachute from the fuselage and clipped it on to Jack's chest. This was the normal procedure, possibly good for morale, but of little value. It was an unwritten law that the pilot stayed at the controls until the crew had jumped. With incredible luck, they might manage to bale out and live, as long as the pilot kept the aircraft on a reasonably even keel. But when the last crew member had jumped there would be no one left. The moment the Pilot released his hold on the controls, K-King would hit the earth long before he could get out of his seat. Nevertheless Les played it according to the book and then clipped on his own parachute from its place on the navigation table. At that moment the port wing fell off, the starboard wing went down, then the nose. In a loud, clear, almost detached voice, our Skipper gave the final command: 'Abandon Aircraft, abandon Aircraft, abandon Aircraft'. And no more.

I staggered to the fuselage, found my parachute, clipped it on to my harness and tried to remember what to do. I was never given the opportunity of even handling a parachute during training, but there was an impressive lecture on what to do if we had to bale out. I vaguely remembered the advice given: 'If you are right-handed you place the lever on the right side. If you jump from the rear exit you should dive head-first as it is easier to replace a foot than a head if you hit the tail plane. Count up to ten and pull.' We were also told that if our parachute harness happened to be slack we would probably break every bone in our body when the parachute opened. We would also land with a very high voice and would be in great demand as a falsetto in the local choir. But before crawling to the rear escape exit I glanced over my shoulder to see our Wireless Operator, Cass Waight, enveloped in flames without his parachute harness. He had been told many times by Jack and Les to wear his harness at all times, but he always refused, saying that it was far too uncomfortable and he could not work in it. It was a terrifying sight.

We were now within minutes or possibly seconds of our crippled plane disintegrating. There was no time for fear and there was so much to be done. A man suddenly faced by the almost certainty of death can be very calm.

I was probably the last crew member to leave the burning bomber which was about to be blown to pieces. The Rear-Gunner, Royston, had already jumped and I had to wait for Mid-Upper Gunner Bolt to go. We were about to jump when both of us, crouched before the now wide-open door, were hit again and we were knocked sprawling against the fuselage. I had the curious sensation of drowning and then lost consciousness. It could only have been for a second or two. When I awoke, Bolt had gone. It was now my turn.

I had great difficulty in getting out, even after Bolt had jumped and cleared the exit. I was forced back on three occasions by the force of the slipstream. I eventually made it, jumped head first, according to instructions, and counted a very hurried ten. After an extempore prayer in Welsh which was both a plea for help and a veiled threat – 'Ein Tad, dyma dy gyfle Di' – I pulled the rip-cord.

I remember falling very rapidly into a black sky, hoping that the earth would come and meet me very quickly and put an end to this uncertainty. A sudden jerk, and the chute opened. It was like stopping still in mid-air. There was no apparent movement and I was quite convinced that I was hanging from the aircraft, and later, when my confused brain started to function, from a church spire.

My portable oxygen bottle and inter-com tube had caught me in the throat, forcing me to look up all the time and I was quite unprepared for a spectacular landing in a small canal between the meadows covered by a thin veneer of ice.

For a few seconds I was not quite sure whether I was in this world or in the next, but a bump on the head, a bloody throat and a twisted ankle convinced me that I was on the good earth. I was alive. I had lost one flying boot on my descent, but with the exception of very trivial and superficial injuries I was completely unharmed and able to walk away. I had prayed in Welsh that if there was a God in Heaven, this was His chance. I now thanked God profusely and hid my parachute.

This is my version of what happened on that disastrous night, but my Navigator, Les, suffered for many years from the recurrent memory of these dramatic events. This was his recall, and I reproduce it as it was written many years later:

'The starboard wing went down, then the nose, and I was half-way down the steps pinned to the fuselage listening to the scream of the Lancaster in a spin. I didn't see any of my life going before my eyes. I can't remember having any thoughts at all. I think I was too scared to do anything but rudely call on God to help me. I seemed to be enveloped in a yellow glow and something like a handrail twisted in front of me. Then there was a flash and I blacked out. When I came round I seemed to be floating on a black velvet cloth covered in diamonds. No sensation of falling; nothing but peaceful quietness. How long this went on I have no idea. I think I tried to turn on the velvet cloth on my elbow, but there was no reaction as if my elbow had gone right through it. The diamonds were slowly moving round, and a feeling of coldness seemed to strike me. I came round fast. I was in a free fall. The diamonds were stars. It was very, very cold. I was out of the plane. Had I really got out of that plane? I had no problems in moving my arms and I brought my right arm to my chest and groped and clawed where the ripcord should be. I was clawing on canvas. Even now I didn't seem to feel scared and reasoned that I must have clipped the chute the wrong way round. I brought my left hand up and there was the cord – oh beautiful bit of frozen metal. I pulled, there was a bit of delay, a loud crack, and I felt as if someone had kicked me in the wedding tackle – hard. I seemed to be swinging in all directions at once, but it slowed down and for an instant I thought I saw a vague white shape like another chute below me. I tried to steer myself towards it but lost it almost immediately, and in any case I had forgotten what to pull on the shrouds. My straps had always been terribly slack and used to fall off my shoulders every time I went down. I had meant to tighten them up sometime. I hung grimly on to the upright webs. I landed mostly on my face in the back yard of a farmhouse. I could not walk as I had injured severely my right leg. I crawled to the front door and knocked.'

Nearly fifty years later I received a phone call from our Flight Engineer, Alex Kibble. I thought that he had perished with the plane and when I asked him how he succeeded in baling out, he replied, 'I didn't – I was blown out'. A total recall in one sentence.

It was a quarter to three on the morning of 20 February, 1944. It was Sunday morning and bitterly cold. There was no evidence of the burning Lancaster and I had no idea what had happened to the other members of the crew. I only knew that Don Bolt had baled out.

I was very much alone and very much alive in an open field somewhere in Europe. I was not quite sure whether I had landed in Germany or in the Netherlands, but almost certain that it was somewhere on the border between the two countries.

I wrapped my parachute and some of my outer flying clothes in a bundle, placed a large stone in it and threw the lot into the canal. I kept the brown overall which had kept me warm at twenty thousand feet, tore off the electric attachments and hoped that I could pass as a labourer. I tried to put into practice the advice given by an Intelligence Officer at the Operational Training Unit at Hixon near Stafford. We were told that the German soldiers would search for any survivors for about three days and that we should keep out of sight for this period. Using the little compass which was concealed inside my collar stud, I started walking away from the wreckage, with one flying boot and a pair of slippers which a few hours previously had been electrically heated.

My immediate reaction was one of gratitude, almost euphoria, at being alive and unhurt. This lasted for an hour or so until I heard our planes returning after completing their mission. They were on the way home and the boys would soon be enjoying their bacon and eggs and possibly another night in Louth. My gratitude was tempered by annoyance and wretched helplessness.

I walked until day-break and then found a convenient hiding place in a large abandoned irrigation pipe. I crawled in and opened for the first time the well-planned RAF escape pack which all bomber crewmen carried in their tunic pocket. This imaginative and functional pack contained a bar of concentrated chocolate, a luminous compass, a metal file, silk maps of Western Europe and paper money in French, Dutch and Belgian notes. All that was necessary to get back home. I never had the opportunity to use the metal file.

I ate a small piece of chocolate and went to sleep. I did not leave my sheltered pipe until late evening when I continued walking until daybreak. This time my temporary home was an isolated barn with plenty of straw in it, and as an added bonus sugar-beet had been dumped in a corner. This supplemented what was left of my concentrated chocolate and there was no shortage of rain water.

On the evening of the 23rd I decided that I had walked far enough away from the crashed aircraft to find out my exact location. There had been very little activity in this rural region. There were no troop movements and I only saw one party of German soldiers and an occasional farm worker in the distance. There was an unnatural silence. I was reasonably confident that I was in Holland.

Three days went by, and I was now beginning to feel hungry and very cold. After watching a small farmhouse for a few hours, and having made quite sure that there were no Germans in the area, I decided to try my luck. Dogs barked and eventually a nervous-looking farmer appeared. It was obvious that I was not a welcome visitor and must have looked a sight. I stared at him and he stared at me. We both spoke but what we said appeared to be incomprehensible. I remember saying, 'Churchill, Wilhelmina, Kamerad', and after much hesitation he beckoned me into the house. There was a complete lack of communication. I produced my escape map and he pointed to the province of Groningen. I was in the Netherlands, about forty kilometres from the German border. After a few minutes, the farmer was joined by his wife and children. Nobody spoke. They were afraid and were fully aware of the dangers of harbouring an allied airman. The penalty would be imprisonment, possibly death. I made a great fuss of the children, kissed the baby, gave the children English money as souvenirs, the mother my silk flying gloves and the farmer a ten guilder note. In return I was given an old pair of shoes and something to eat and drink. My reluctant host had two options: to carry out the instructions of the German authorities and report my arrival and receive a 'good conduct' mark, or conceal me during a period of intense German activity, as by now the wreckage would have been found together with the bodies of some members of the crew. He did neither, but hastily got rid of me by taking me to a neighbouring farm a few fields away. With a sigh of relief at having solved his immediate problem, he hastily returned to his home and left me with a family of unquestionable loyalty.

At this second farm the gradual process of becoming a Dutchman began. My RAF uniform was exchanged for a blue peasant smock called a *kiel*, an old pair of black-striped trousers, a black hat and a pair of wooden clogs. My greatest acquisition was a splendid old-fashioned lady's bicycle with a vicious 'backpedal' brake. At midnight on the following night I cycled behind the farmer in the semi-darkness, keeping a distance of about four hundred yards between us. There were regular military road obstructions and I twice fell off this ancient contraption. We arrived at the home of his brother-in-law at six o'clock in the morning, confident that I was now in good hands and that I would not be betrayed. At this hospitable home on the outskirts of a village I was introduced to a young girl called Betsy. There had not been time during the past few hectic days for a proper wash and there were still traces of oil and dried blood on my face. Betsy took one look at me and said, 'You poor brave English Tommy,' (British airmen were known in the Netherlands as 'Tommies' and the Germans as 'Moffen') and asked me to speak in whispers as there were children asleep upstairs. They were the children of a young woman from Rotterdam and were suffering from malnutrition.

It was far too dangerous to remain in this house and in the early hours of the morning Betsy's father brought me to the village schoolmaster who was working for the Resistance. Together we cycled on unmade roads and dirt tracks to one of the most isolated farmsteads in the Province where I remained with an unmarried farmer for a day or two, before taking to the road once again.

It was Sunday, 27 February. I cycled on a cold, crisp morning, with church bells ringing, to a small farm a few kilometres away, where I was hidden for two days. I was to enjoy the luxury of having a boiled egg for breakfast and was taken into a barn, where a perfectly innocent-looking hayrick had a door in it camouflaged by straw, concealing a powerful radio and a large map of Europe. I listened to the news in English from the BBC.

As we sat talking, two military-looking men, in what appeared to be a German uniform, walked in unannounced. I thought the game was up, and that I had been betrayed. The two men were Dutch policemen, patriotic members of the Resistance.

One of the policemen produced a little heart made of perspex which he had found in the inside pocket of the mutilated body of a member of the crew of the Lancaster before the German search party had arrived. The letters SA were incribed on the heart, and there was also a 'South Africa' flash on his inside tunic. I was able to tell him that it belonged to our Skipper, Jack Laurens. He also informed me that they had found the body of another airman with an unopened parachute in the same area, and, a few kilometres away from the crash, the body of a 'coloured' airman, badly burnt, and also without a chute. The first was Bolt and the second Waight.

At midnight on the second day I cycled to the town of Leek

and made my first contact with the official Underground movement. I was escorted by my two policemen friends to the home of the Head of the Resistance in the area. He was the headmaster of the Christian school who introduced himself as Mr Janson. All members of the Resistance gave false names for security reasons. (Janson was probably the equivalent of Jones in Wales!) I met his wife and we had cake, coffee and cigars. The Gestapo were suspicious of him and he never slept in his own home. I spent the night with one of his neighbours and was given a great welcome with even a hot-water bottle in my bed. Trams passed by the window advertising Persil and German soldiers passed by on the other side.

After cigarettes and coffee I was given a thorough grilling. At that time the Germans were dropping their own agents in RAF uniform to penetrate the Underground movement. He asked me a number of technical questions which could only have been answered by a member of the Royal Air Force. I was asked, for example, to describe the so-called 'Laminetta' method, known to us as 'Window', in which bundles of tinfoil were dropped in large quantities and which formed a wall which could not be penetrated by the German radar rays, and which blocked the German radar screen. I was able to satisfy him, and was taken into his study. He took a copy of the Koran from a shelf in his library; the inside was hollow, and in this holy book he kept all his Resistance reports.

He had intense hatred of the Germans and showed me a photograph of some of his friends who had been shot by the SS as reprisals for obstructing the passage of German troops. About thirty were shot, though many of them had nothing to do with the event. He promised to help me and said that he would try to get me home in three or four weeks. It was a wonderful thought.

When I left, 'Mijnheer Janson' asked me whether I had a hat, and when I said no he gave me his own. When I tried to thank him, he said, 'You must not thank us. We cannot fight and you are doing it for us.'

That night, after curfew, I cycled with the two policemen for a few kilometres until we came to a car with the engine running in readiness for us. Eventually we arrived in the town of Oosterwolde in Friesland and to a farm called 'Romsicht', the home of the delightful Tiesinga family.

These are of necessity rather vague recollections of my first fortnight in Occupied Europe. I did not know the names of the friends who helped me, nor have any idea of my exact location, nor the distances covered at night. My only aim was to get as far as possible from the wreckage and the search area without being detected, and hopefully to get home.

Seventy-nine aircraft failed to return from the Leipzig mission in the early hours of Sunday, 20 February, 1944. There were over 553 empty beds on the various squadrons, and 553 telegrams to the next of kin: 'I regret to inform you that your son is missing after an operation. Letter will follow'.

The next days and weeks were periods of intense anxiety for parents and wives. In my case the uncertainty and suspense lasted for over six months. I had not been killed or taken prisoner, and there could be no communication.

The letter which Herky posted to my parents was in an envelope marked 'Strictly Confidential' and they received it on 22 February, together with a letter from the Squadron. I recently came across my own letter and also letters from the parents of my missing crew and Jack's wife, as my mother had corresponded regularly with them in the hope that one of them would hear something of our fate. In my letter I begged my parents to be as brave and realistic as possible, pointed out that quite a number of us would be taken prisoner and would be well treated, as there were many German prisoners in the United Kingdom. I then tried to justify my membership of aircrew, and wrote: 'When I joined the RAF it was with the one intention of flying, not because I was particularly interested in flying as such, but because in this capacity I could do my best. I have known all along what I was in for and I would have it no other way. I have endeavoured to live as full a life as possible and it has been a happy one. I had always hoped and dreamed of repaying you for everything you have done for me; giving me a good home and a good education. I do appreciate it all and I am sorry I have not had the opportunity of having this dream realized.' I then made a plea to my brother, Nefydd, who was seventeen, to help them in every possible way.

The letter on p. 36 was from the Squadron.

The only other letter from the Squadron wad dated 10 March, informing my father that my personal effects had been dispatched to the Central Depository, RAF Colnbrook, Slough. From now on Royal Air Force bureaucracy took over and another five letters from the Central Depository followed. On 13 March my father was asked to fill in a form of indemnity 'duly signed and witnessed' and on 5 May my personal effects were dispatched to Boncath by passenger train. All this unnecessary activity for the rather pathetic contents of a kitbag did nothing to improve morale at home. I only wish they could have kept them for another month. The one item of value, a gold wrist watch, was not returned.

In the Squadron letter of 21 February the Wing Commander said that my father 'would be immediately advised on any further information that is received'. The second letter did not arrive until 30 June, and this time from the Air Ministry, an insensitive letter from a civil servant in Oxford Street, which, like the personal effects letters, only caused greater anxiety, especially the unfortunate phrase 'action to presume that he has lost his life will not be taken until evidence of his death is received'. (See p. 37)

There were frequent letters between Mrs Margaret Laurens, the parents of Bolt, Burton, Royston and Kibble, and my mother, from March until August, 1944. These letters are very revealing and reflect the hopes and frustrations, and at times the helplessness of the writers during these months of uncertainty.

Margaret's first letter was written on 26 April and mirrors the feelings of most of the parents: 'This tension is awful but we must be brave for their sakes. My little boy and I were staying at Ludford at the time and waved goodbye.'

Again on 16 June she wrote to say that she had visited the

Royal Air Force Station,
Ludford Magna,
Market Rasen,
Lincs.

21st February, 1944.

101S/C.509/133/11.

Dear Mr. Davies,

        I am writing to offer you the sincere sympathy both of myself and the entire Squadron in the anxiety you have experienced since hearing that your Son, 1651898 Sergeant J. A. Davies, is missing from Air Operations on the Night of the 19/20th February, 1944.

        The aircraft in which your Son was a member of the Crew took off on an operational Sortie over enemy territory, but I regret to say failed to return to base. No messages were received from the aircraft after take off and nothing has so far been heard of it or any member of the Crew.

        There is always the possibility that they may have come down by parachute or made a forced landing in enemy territory, in which case news of this would take a considerable time to come through, but you will be immediately advised of any further information that is received.

        Your Son had been with us for only a short time, but I was very much impressed by the keenness and efficiency he displayed in his work and I had great hopes for his future with the Squadron.

        The personal effects of your Son are now in the custody of the "Committee of Adjustment Officer, R.A.F. Station, Ludford Magna", who will be writing to you shortly concerning their disposal.

        It is desired to explain that the request in the telegram notifying you of the casualty to your Son, was included with the object of avoiding his chance of escape being prejudiced by undue publicity in case he was still at large. This is not to say that any information about him is available, but is a precaution adopted in the case of all personnel reported missing.

        I feel most deeply for you in this anxious time, and we all join with you in hoping and praying that your Son is safe.

Yours sincerely,

R. I. Alexander,
Wing Commander, Commanding,
No. 101 Squadron, R.A.F.

Mr. H. C. Davies,
"Bryn - Hedydd",
Boncath,
Pembrokeshire.

36

Any communications on the
subject of this letter should
be addressed to :—
        THE
UNDER SECRETARY
    OF STATE,
and the following number
quoted :—

Your Ref. ..P.413938/8/P.4.(B.6)

AIR MINISTRY

(Casualty Branch),

73-77, OXFORD STREET

W.

3O June 1944

Sir,

I am directed to inform you, with deep regret,
that all efforts to trace your son, 1651898 Sergeant
J. A. Davies, have proved unavailing.

In view of the absence of news for so long a
period, it is felt that you should be informed of this
Department's grave anxiety for his safety, but action to
presume that he has lost his life will not be taken until
evidence of his death is received, or until such time has
elapsed that it is considered there can be no longer any
likelihood of his survival.

Such action will then be for official purposes
only and will not be taken until this Department has
communicated with you further.

I am to assure you that all possible enquiries
are continuing.

I am, Sir,
    Your obedient Servant,

for Director of Personal Services.

H. G. Davies Esq.,
    Bryn-Hedydd,
        Boncath,
            Pembrokeshire.

Squadron but that there was no news and 'It takes me all my time to concentrate on anything. I have heard from my husband's people in South Africa. They have not seen Jack for eight years and I am afraid they are taking the news very badly. My little boy and I are quite well. I only received my husband's personal belongings this week.'

All the parents wrote early in April to express their joy that news had been received that Rear-Gunner Royston was alive and in a prison camp in Germany. He was an only son and his father in a letter on 2 June said that when he heard the news he had become dizzy and had fallen into the fireplace and had cracked a few ribs. His doctor said that it was a reaction from the suspense.

Mr Kibble, in a letter of 19 April, put everything into some kind of perspective. Before opening the telegram on 20 February he wondered whether it was news about Alex in the RAF or his only other son who was on active service with the Royal Artillery in the front line of the action in Italy. Three days later, on 23 February, a stick of bombs landed on their home in Chelsea. Mr and Mrs Kibble had a miraculous escape but lost most of their home. He was not seriously hurt but was buried up to his chest in débris and was rescued after two hours with only a few cuts and bruises and damaged legs. He ended his letter with these comforting words: 'As I was rescued the thought came to me that God had spared me so that I might see my son again. I felt a little more confident that our lad would be among those saved, including your son.' On 4 June he wrote to say that he and his wife were now fully recovered from the bombing and had settled down in a new home in Elm Park Gardens, Chelsea.

Mrs Burton corresponded regularly and after the first few months her letters were full of hope for the future. In the early days she was rather depressed and in April she wrote: 'Owing to the worry I have decided to take up some other work outside'.

There were long and cheerful letters from Mrs Bolt who was confident until the very end that her son was alive. Don, who was 22 on the 1st of February, was her only son and this was his twenty-third trip over Germany, including fourteen to Berlin. She listened carefully to the German news every other evening from 7.15 until 8.30 as William Joyce, christened Lord Haw-Haw, in a propaganda programme called 'Germany Calling' announced the names of a number of airmen who were prisoners or who had been killed over Germany. Early in July Mr and Mrs Bolt received the dreaded telegram from the Air Ministry to say that they had heard from the International Red Cross that Donald was believed killed and was laid to rest at the cemetery in Tolbert in the parish of Leek, which is nine miles from Groningen. Mrs Bolt was alone in the house when the telegram arrived as her husband was on night duty. She received the following translation of a letter from the Minister of the Church in Leek on 3 August: 'In order not to leave you too long in anxiety, I answer your letter of the third as soon as possible. As all my household are ill and I have no servant I am writing in Dutch. Although I understand English it is possible that if I had to write in a hurry I might make many mistakes and I think there will be someone near you who can translate this letter. May I begin by sending you my sincere condolences in the loss of your only son. I understand that sorrow is with you although I can understand that you are proud your son had died in a fight for right and justice. He and his pilot, Jack Laurens, were buried in the church cemetery at Tolbert which is the cemetery of the Dutch Reformed Church in this place. On the night of the 19/20 February, 1944, the plane in which your son was crashed just outside our village and the German troops of occupation went immediately to the place where the disaster happened. The remains of the aeroplane and the bodies of both the fliers were protected by them. On 20 February in the afternoon I asked permission to go to the place where their mortal remains were at that time. This was permitted to my wife and myself. On 22 February at 11 o'clock in the morning the Mayor of the Commune Leek asked me to take the funeral. I agreed and asked him in which language it should be done and he replied "in Dutch".

'When my wife and I arrived at the cemetery there were hundreds of people there to pay honour to the dead. Upon the orders of the German military who were present one of the four Dutch policemen had to order the people who were there out of the cemetery, but my wife, a deaconess and a friend of ours would not allow themselves to be driven out. The Burgomaster also remained. I asked to speak by the side of the grave but this was not permitted. I was only allowed to act as clergyman. I used by the graveside the service of our Church which is very similar to the Anglican service and I spoke from the text 1st Corinthians 15, 1/57: "Thanks be to God who has given us the victory through Jesus Christ our Lord".

'The following day flowers were brought to the grave by the people and it is the intention to bring flowers again to the grave on August 18 when we are celebrating our festival of liberation.

'On the 22nd July I read your letter in my Church.'

The remainder of the letter is missing. The *Dominee* (minister) was not permitted to speak by the side of the grave, but Don and Jack had a Christian burial and the text from the Scriptures was not challenged. This was not the experience of the priests conducting the burial service of the allied airmen killed on the raid on the secret research establishment at Peenemunde in August, 1943, when, according to Martin Middlebrook in *The Peenemunde Raid*, a Luftwaffe Major told the two clergymen: 'Gentlemen, if you try to preach about that Jewish lout, Jesus, I will immediately order the troops to march off'. The Reading referred to the Christian belief in the Resurrection, but as the Major tried to carry out his threat, an Admiral intervened and shouted, 'Soldiers stand fast, Vicar please continue'. There were serious moral conflicts inside the Germany of the Third Reich.

All the parents were loud in their praise of the help they received from the International Red Cross. On 5 May, 1945, the 'Wounded, Missing and Relatives Department of the British Red Cross Society and Order of St John of Jerusalem' wrote to my mother to say that they were doing everything possible to obtain news about me. Eventually on 3 August, 1944, another

GERRARD 9234

TELEPHONE:
Extn. 3801

Any communications on the
subject of this letter should
be addressed to :—
THE
UNDER SECRETARY
OF STATE.
and the following number
quoted :— F.413938/8/P.3.

Your Ref. ....

AIR MINISTRY

(Casualty Branch),

73-77, OXFORD STREET,

W.1.

3rd August, 1944.

CONFIDENTIAL

Sir,

      I am directed to refer to a letter from this Department
dated the 30th June, 1944, and to advise you that information
has been received that your son, Sergeant James Arthur Davies,
Royal Air Force, landed in occupied territory and is alive and
well.

      In the interests of your son and his benefactors you
are asked to keep this good news to yourself and not ask for
further information or attempt to communicate with him in any
way. It should be appreciated that if your son is caught it
not only means that he will become a prisoner of war but that
those harbouring him will no doubt serve the death penalty. In
these circumstances it is felt sure that you will co-operate.

      Any more definite news will be passed to you immediately
it is received.

                I am, Sir,
                Your obedient Servant,

                    S. L. Baker

         for Director of Personal Services.

H. G. Davies, Esq.,
    Bryn-Hedydd,
      Boncath,
        Pembrokeshire.

letter was sent by the Air Ministry informing my parents that I had landed in occupied territory and was alive and well. They were asked to keep the good news to themselves. My mother immediately wrote to the other parents of the crew to tell them.

The last letter from the Air Ministry arrived on 6 November, 1944, to state that action was now being taken officially to reclassify me as a Prisoner of War.

But I am digressing and must return to my movements since leaving on a gas-fuelled ancient American car to an unknown destination.

CHAPTER THREE

FRIESLAND

The term 'Resistance' in this section is in a way misleading, as these recollections add very little to what has already been written on the organization of the Resistance movements in Occupied Europe. These words have been written with some sense of urgency, before it is too late, in order to record the incredible courage of these lifelong friends who hid me for six months during the German Occupation of their country. Perhaps this *'petite histoire'* will illustrate some of the larger issues which have already been recorded by the official historians of the Resistance. M. R. D. Foot, in his authoritative book *Resistance*, has examined in detail the organization of the Underground movements in Europe, and under the heading 'What Happened' has dealt fully with the Resistance movements in the Netherlands and in Belgium.

Unfortunately some of my unsung heroes are no longer with us, but their sons and daughters are deeply conscious of the sacrifices made by their parents, and this is an inadequate expression of thanks.

Most of my Resistance friends evaded capture, though some had to go into hiding for long periods, and others were imprisoned. They carried out their pre-war occupations as farmers, office-workers, Protestant pastors and Catholic priests, journalists, butchers, schoolmasters and factory owners. The Resistance was a great unifying force in which the Protestant peasant farmer from Friesland and the well-heeled Catholic industrialist from Brabant combined forces, possibly for the first time.

Germany had refused to respect Dutch neutrality and on 10

May, 1940, early in the morning, with no declaration of war, the full weight of the Wehrmacht was unleashed on the Netherlands. On 14 May much of Rotterdam was destroyed by air bombardment. The Dutch were forced to capitulate and Queen Wilhelmina and her family crossed to England where a Government in exile was formed.

According to the Dutch historian Dr Lou de Jong, rivalry between the different branches of the British Secret Service operating in London in the early 1940s led to the arrest of almost all the Dutch agents they sent out to the Netherlands and to the deaths of many members of Dutch Resistance groups. In the period between March, 1941, and July, 1942, of the eleven agents sent out by M16, eight were arrested, one killed and two succeeded in returning to England. Of the nineteen agents sent out by SOE sixteen were arrested, seven immediately after they were parachuted into the Netherlands, two were killed and one managed to return. All the evidence suggests that the lack of security training for the agents meant that they led the German occupying forces directly to the Dutch Resistance movements. The Germans set up what was known as the *Englandspiel*, as various radio operators were arrested complete with all their codes and were persuaded, in exchange for promises that the lives of friends or fellow agents would be spared, to transmit messages back to SOE and to act as though they were continuing their activities.

There were other difficulties in organizing an effective Resistance in the Netherlands. M. R. D. Foot reminds us that in comparison with all other German occupied countries, the Netherlands was geographically at a serious disadvantage, as other countries bordered on neutral zones and their couriers could reach Switzerland, Spain or Sweden. The Netherlands was isolated and it was comparatively easy for the Germans to maintain complete control. The landscape also created problems as it was difficult to drop agents by parachute or to land them by Lysander aircraft in this flat, densely-populated and sparsely-wooded country.

For five years the Dutch people experienced the full horrors of German occupation, but in spite of the difficulties mentioned, it was a period of gallant resistance.

As far as I know, my Resistance friends did not blow up bridges, derail German troop trains, or become actively involved in the dramatic acts of sabotage which made the headlines, though some of them were prepared to do so. They were, nevertheless, fully aware of the penalties if caught working for the Resistance. Over 10,000 Dutchmen and Dutchwomen died at German hands for their part in the struggle.

To come back to Oosterwolde. It was daybreak when we arrived at 'Romsicht', a word in the Frisian language meaning 'Wide Horizons'. I was received with great warmth by the farmer and his wife, De Heer and Mevrouw Lambert Tiesinga, and later met their three young children, two little boys, Chemi and Andreas, and a baby girl called Tiny. They had a servant boy working for them, but for security reasons I was not allowed to see him. Their maid, Chokie, on the other hand, was older, could be trusted and was fully aware of my identity.

Another two boys were also being hidden by Lambert: Klaas Westra from Weiss, and Daio Van der Meer from Kampen, Dutch boys who had been there since the start of the German occupation in order to avoid being forced to work in Germany; like many other young men from the south of the Netherlands they went 'Underground' in rural Friesland.

In the 1940s Romsicht was an isolated farm on the outskirts of Oosterwolde and any visitors could easily be seen long before they approached the house. Tall plants were placed on the window sill of my small room in order to prevent anyone from looking in. I felt very secure in this hospitable home. The first few days were ones of uncertainty and inactivity. There was no contact with the Resistance and there was nothing to do except to sit near the window and absorb my immediate environment – flat polders, canals, windmills and waterways, and the sailing ships which seemed to be cruising over the fields. My imagination was in overdrive and I planned highly successful escapes.

In the evening at about eight o'clock the servant boy went home and the children went to bed. At this magic hour I would join my hosts, Chokie, Klaas and Daio in front of the large peat-burning stove and listen to the good Vrouw playing their favourite hymns on a small organ. These pleasant evenings would come to an end with Mrs Tiesinga's rendering of 'God Save the King'.

A few neighbours came every morning at eleven o'clock to listen to the BBC European Service, on a radio cunningly concealed behind a picture of Millet's 'Angelus'.

On dark evenings I was allowed to go with Klaas and Daio for a walk in the fields and once they showed me with pride their 'dugout' which was neatly constructed and contained a small bed. This was their hiding place whenever the Germans made a raid, as it was surrounded by water and the tracker dogs lost the scent.

One day an elderly gentleman came into my room and said in halting English, 'I am the Reverend'. He was a member of the Resistance and came to see me once or twice, bringing with him some books by Edgar Wallace and the New Testament in English. This helped considerably and for the first time in my life I read the New Testament in English from cover to cover, many times over.

Another welcome visitor was Klaas's father. He came from Weiss to see his son and gave me a box of good cigars as a present, a rare luxury as tobacco was severely rationed and good cigars very difficult to obtain.

Perhaps I should explain why I have emphasized that I was now in Friesland and not in Holland. On being introduced to the Tiesinga family, I expressed my gratitude and my relief on being hidden in Holland instead of surviving in a camp in Germany. I was gently reprimanded and was told in no uncertain terms that I was now in Friesland and that Holland was only one of the eleven historic provinces in the Kingdom of the Netherlands. *'Meneer, wij zijn verschillende mensen en wij hebben een verschillende taal'* – we are different people and we have a different language. We are Netherlands and not

Hollanders. I can quite understand this, as I, a Welshman, had previously been accused of being a poor English Tommy!

The Frisian language was spoken by some 250,000 people, with a literature of its own, as well as many translations into Frisian. It has been claimed that the Saxon invaders of Britain were Frisian adventurers, a suggestion supported by the affinity between the Frisian and the English languages. The following example requires no translation – 'Let us nou de warld forjitte', but an unfriendly world could not be ignored in German-occupied Friesland. My good friend and former courier, Tiny Mulder, a writer and a poet in the Frisian language, has played an active part in the recognition of the language in the schools and in the community.

Lambert, the courteous and dignified head of the family was deeply involved in the Resistance, though his wife had only a vague idea of his underground activities at the time. She was fully occupied looking after her young children, but at all times radiated a quiet confidence and tremendous serenity.

Mealtimes were formal occasions, when Lambert, the gentle Church deacon, prayed for our safety, the liberation of his beloved Friesland and then read a chapter from the Bible.

The family were in great danger, especially during the last months of the war, when I was told that in April, 1945, Lambert was forced to leave his wife and children and go underground in Drachten. Weapons and ammunition had been hidden under 'terps' on his land – manmade earthen mounds thrown up perhaps over two thousand years ago before the construction of the dykes as a protection against flood water. Lambert had been betrayed by a German collaborator, and was hidden by the Resistance until the liberation. Vrouw Tiesinga was now on her own, with the responsibility of looking after the farm, as well as her young family.

During the last few weeks of the Occupation, the Germans stole her horses, and she was ordered to hand over her pigs and take them to Leeuwarden. She refused.

Centuries of struggle against nature and foreign domination had resulted in a people conscious of their individuality and independence; inheritors of a proud tradition. Central Frisia, now the province of Friesland, was a reluctant signatory of the Union of Utrecht in 1579 by choosing its own Stadholders, and it was not surprising that the present inhabitants refused to be bullied by Seyess-Inquart, the man the German Führer appointed as Reich-Commissioner for the Netherlands in 1940.

After about a fortnight an attractive 22-year-old girl named Tiny Mulder came to see me. She was the courier for the Resistance and it appeared that since the end of 1943 she had been asked to assume responsibility for allied airmen who had crashed over a fairly large area of northern Netherlands. In an article written in the Frisian language, Tiny described vividly the day in which her country was invaded and her immediate reaction to the capitulation of the Dutch army:

'May 10, 1940. Daybreak. I am awakened by a steady, almost lazy drone of aeroplanes going from east to west. I get up and look through my bedroom window. Our village, Drachten, is still asleep, nowhere any lights, but then we are used to blackout since September, 1939. The blossoms of our apple trees shine snow white in the still lingering darkness of the night. War. Germany attacks the Netherlands. I am nineteen.

'May 14, 1940. The Netherlands forces capitulate. Occupation. How to find a new equilibrium in totally different circumstances than we had been used to? How to interpret the messages and measures of the German authorities? I despise them, but how to express that feeling? One thing was clear from the very beginning: only a small percentage of the Dutch people embraced Nazi ideology. At first people showed their aversion by simple means such as wearing an orange flower on their coats on August 31, Queen Wilhelmina's birthday. Some were taken to jail, but not for long.'

Then, as the weeks went by, I learnt her story. In the summer Tiny accepted an invitation from by Mr Pieter Wijbenga to become a member of his staff. He was the Director of the Distribution Office in Drachten, the bureau that organized the distribution of food and clothing. She soon realized that the

Director had been very careful in selecting his personnel and that no one with Nazi sympathies would be tolerated in a bureau which was ideally placed as a centre for Resistance activities. He made his intentions quite clear in the spring of 1942 when he informed Tiny that he was engaged in espionage activities for the allied forces and asked her whether she would be willing to help, since there would be more and more illegal activities in the years ahead. She willingly and enthusiastically agreed, and that was the beginning of her invaluable work for the Resistance.

There were four distinct phases to her underground activities. Initially it meant working with three or four people in Drachten to help Jewish people avoid deportation to what were known as 'Work force camps in Poland'. Their real destination was still unknown, but there were growing suspicions, especially when very old Jews and people with physical and mental handicaps were deported. A number of them were advised to go into hiding. Students in Amsterdam were active at this time in saving Jewish children from the hands of the enemy and quite a number of Jews were brought to Friesland. Tiny assisted in the work of finding families who were able and willing to take one or more Jews to their homes and then accompanying them to their hiding places. They had to be provided with new, false identity cards with non-Jewish names and without the big black J that was printed on their original identity cards. The carefully screened staff in the Distribution Bureau willingly provided ration coupons for the holders of these false cards.

The second phase involved helping the growing army of men who were forced to work in Germany but who refused to help the enemy. They also had to be found safe hiding places and provided with false papers and ration coupons.

Tiny was now well integrated into the work of the Resistance and the third phase included courier work all over the Netherlands, transporting letters, secret documents and occasionally small arms. This was all carried out after office hours and on weekends.

Mr Wijbenga had absolute faith in Tiny and when he created

a KP (Knok Ploeg) unit within the Resistance she was again asked to carry out courier work for the unit, such as transporting stolen ration coupons. The KP was a unit of five or six men who were armed and committed raids on town halls, distribution offices and Employment Bureaus which organized the search for workers who should be in Germany. As a result of these raids, blank identity cards and ration coupons were stolen and the Registers of Population together with the Register for Able Men were destroyed.

All this activity had taken place before we met in Garijp, when she became the courier for allied airmen who were hiding in the Province. This was highly dangerous and from March, 1944, she had been warned that she was on the Gestapo black list, and that her life was in danger. She therefore went into hiding herself and operated from different villages and from different farms.

Early in 1944 she received a warning that German intelligence had sent some of their people in American uniform, and speaking American perfectly, to penetrate the ranks of the helpers of allied airmen. Whenever an airman had not been seen baling out of an aircraft, and there was no sign in the vicinity of a crashlanding or of a parachute, the airman had to be rigorously screened. This was a difficult undertaking as the airmen had about as much reason to distrust this unknown girl as she had of them. Tiny had to ask many questions, some regarding highly classified air force secrets. One airman became so suspicious that he threatened her. He was interrogated in the house of a colleague where the airman had found temporary shelter. She left him and returned with an armed friend who posted himself outside the door of the room where she continued her interrogation. The man was a genuine Canadian airman.

Before the end of 1943 Tiny and her organization had succeeded in taking a few airmen to the coast, and from there back to England, sometimes by submarine. When the route became too difficult they were sent via Sweden. Later still another change had to be made as the Swedish route had become too risky, so the airmen had to be sent through Belgium and France down to the Pyrenees where smugglers and shepherds who knew every mountain track took them to neutral Spain. Here they reported to the British Embassy in Madrid, with every hope of being shipped or flown home. This was the plan, and this was to have been my route. There followed many weeks of active preparation.

In April, 1944, one of Tiny's colleagues, a reporter on a rival Leeuwarden newspaper was imprisoned in Leeuwarden. He had stolen a machine gun and ammunition from the German airfield, but was able to conceal them before being seen by the German security guards. He was arrested and charged with acting suspiciously, and for being on a military airfield without authority. His defence was that he was only there to steal petrol, and that he was not in any way connected with the theft of the machine gun. There was considerable tension between the Luftwaffe and the Gestapo in the area and, because of this, according to the prisoner, the theft of the machine gun was kept quiet and was not reported to the Gestapo. The name of the prisoner was Jildert Sudema and, shortly after the war ended, Tiny Mulder became Mrs Sudema.

The local Resistance was very active and efficient during this period and a well-organized rescue operation to release the prisoners from Leeuwarden jail was entirely successful. Not a shot was fired, no one was injured and all the imprisoned Resistance fighters managed to escape. They were taken out of the immediate area and were hidden until the liberation of the Netherlands.

When the war ended, Jildert was present as a newspaper reporter at the trial of the NSB (National Socialist Party) collaborators and the Landwacht, when he recognized the man who had marched him from the airfield to the prison.

Although I was only with the Tiesinga family for a few weeks, I shall always remember them for their bravery, kindness and love, and I was sorry that for security reasons I had to leave. Before doing so, Lambert presented me with a farewell present, a little pipe with an aircraft embossed on the china bowl. It was in constant use for the next six months.

I was later to learn from a member of the Resistance that the reason for my leaving Oosterwolde was that the servant boy could not be trusted and that he had been overheard boasting in a cafe in the town that there was an airman hiding in the farm. A few years ago Vrouw Tiesinga came to stay with us in our home in Beaumaris and, though she had never been told the truth behind the decision to move me from the farm, she vehemently denied the charge that the servant had acted irresponsibly. It now appears that the true reason for the move was that it was becoming far too dangerous to stay in the Oosterwolde area for longer than a few weeks as there was increased German activity in the district, and the Resistance had to try to find safer hiding places. It was also pointed out by Tiny that the policy of the local Resistance group was to try to concentrate as many evaders as possible in the Drachten area so that they could be in easy reach of the couriers who had to travel everywhere on bicycles.

All the necessary arrangements had been made and in the early hours of the morning a car arrived at the farm and an active member of the Resistance known by the name of Jopie came to meet me. He was incredibly brave and not very bright. I said goodbye to my hosts in Romsicht, quite confident that I would be home in a few weeks time.

There were very few cars on the roads in Friesland during the Occupation, and it was said that the only people who used them at that time were Germans and men of the Resistance.

I travelled with Jopie in an ancient car fitted with a huge gas container on the roof. I took out my compass and noticed that we were heading towards the coast, but after a few hours we arrived at the village of Garijp, only about ten kilometres from Leeuwarden, the provincial capital.

A short man with unruly red hair and a thick growth of beard introduced himself as Pieter Dijkstra, the head of the family, and then presented his wife, Hinke, a large and impressive lady wearing a coarse, shapeless dress and a pair of clogs. To complete this rather bizarre scenario in the twilight, she was holding a dangerous looking carving knife. A few minutes later

10. Pieter's 'partner and trusted friend, Bill Deknatel' (*p 52*).

11. Van der Val, the village butcher (*see p 60*).

12. The Dijkstra house in Garijp. The trapdoor to the cellar is just inside the front door.

13. The author (*front*) with Ruurd Postma on his motor-cycle (*see p 62*).

14. Three men in a boat. The author is on the le[ft] (*see p 71*).

15. Simon and Dina de Cock with their four children (*see p 83*).

16. Simon and Dina in 1983 wearing their Resistance decorations.

17. 'My new hosts, Mr and Mrs Fernand Staquet' (*p 96*).

18. Lucy Luyten-Staquet (*see p 96*) Mme Fernand Rahier, 'who on several occasions sheltered allied airmen' (*p 97*), and the author.

we were joined by Elisabeth, their nine-year-old daughter, but looking much older than her tender years.

We sat down in the scantily furnished *voorkamer*, and the first question I asked in the few words of Dutch which I had mastered was, 'How long do I stay with you before going home?' Pieter shrugged his shoulders and put up his hand showing five fingers. 'Five days,' I said with glee, 'Nein,' he said, 'but perhaps five weeks'. He should have said five long months.

I was given a bowl of *'supen groattenbrij'* a kind of porridge made from sour milk. I was violently sick.

CHAPTER FOUR

FIVE LONG MONTHS
IN GARIJP

Pieter showed me a ready-made grave in his vegetable garden and an ancient revolver – *mijn wapen* – which was hidden in the cutlery drawer in the kitchen. After telling me that we really should be enemies and not allies, making a reference to the Boer War, this fearless and loyal Dutch resistance fighter told me exactly what was expected of me should there be a raid on the village and a German soldier entered the house. A knowledge of the Dutch language was not necessary to understand his directive; the unfortunate German would have to be shot and buried. Pieter was fully aware of what would happen to his family and took the necessary precautions. He had also bricked off a section of his cellar, the new bricks having been white-washed to match the old ones. He had made a trap-door which opened out onto the wooden floor just inside the front door of the house. It fitted perfectly and was virtually unnoticeable, even when not covered by a mat.

This was not the first occasion for Pieter to become involved in Resistance activities, as he had previously sheltered Jewish girls for a few days on their flight to freedom.

Many young Dutchmen were forced to work in the factories in Germany, and a large number of them had been rounded up by the 'Razzia' and despatched to a transit camp at Vries about 50 kilometres from Garijp. Pieter was not forced to go to work in Germany on health grounds, but his acute stomach pains did not prevent him from cycling to the camp in order to rescue some of these young men. He picked them up when they worked outside the camp and carried them on his bicycle to places outside the reach of the Germans, where they went 'Underground'.

Although Elisabeth was only nine years of age, she was made fully aware of the risks taken by her parents, and what would happen to the three of them if they were caught. She was denied many of the pleasures which a girl of her age had every reason to expect and grew up in a tense and unnatural atmosphere of fear and suspicion. She had been sworn to secrecy and could never discuss the activities which took place in her home with her school friends, or invite any of them home. She was constantly on guard and there was very little joy in her young life. Pieter had prepared for every eventuality and she was told that if, on her way home from school, she saw a German car outside the house, she was to ignore it and go to a house in another part of the village. She always had to carry this address with her, and was told in no uncertain terms that if she entered her own home she would be sent with her parents to a camp and possibly be shot.

Pieter was a full-time employee of the local milk factory and collected daily samples of milk which were to be tested for tuberculosis and fat content, and duly registered. The milking was by hand, so he had to leave the house every morning between 5.30 and 6 o'clock as the testing had to be done on the farms during the milking periods. The same procedure was repeated in the afternoon. In addition to this twice-daily ritual, there was intense activity in our temporary home on the day before market day in Leeuwarden, when farmers arrived in the *achterkamer* for Pieter to sign certificates to state that their cows were free from tuberculosis and that the fat content was satisfactory. This written evidence determined the price which they could expect in the provincial market. On these occasions, and in this small *achterkamer*, Pieter had the authority of a Stadholder, and reigned supreme. When these animated discussions were taking place, I was safely shelling beans upstairs, and when the last farmer left with his authorized documents, I joined my adopted family for the prolonged evening meal.

Pieter had a little land of his own, a few sheep, one cow, and a horse which he shared with his friend, Bill Deknatel. He said that he had no intention of having his own cow tested.

At ten-thirty each morning Pieter came tearing into the house shouting 'Coffee' at the top of his voice. His wife, the gentle and loveable Hinke, was fully prepared for this daily outburst and would have four cups already poured and ready to drink as Pieter did not have the patience to wait for his cup to be refilled. He lived on his nerves during this difficult period, and so did we all. I was very devoted to the saintly Vrouw who only panicked when Pieter was in one of his intemperate moods, a sick man and suffering from severe stomach pains, when the tensions that underlay his peppery crust came to the surface. After his hurried coffee he would make a dramatic exit and we would not see him again until the midday meal.

During my early days in Garijp Pieter introduced me to his partner and trusted friend, Bill Deknatel, who, according to Pieter, spoke good English. Bill greeted me with the words, 'I speak English; I smoke the pipe', his one and only English phrase. He did not even smoke a pipe, but constantly chewed black-market Belgian shag, at ten guilders an ounce, which he spat out at regular intervals into a large mug commemorating the enthronement of Queen Wilhelmina. It was always a pleasure to meet Bill on his frequent visits, a delightful, uncomplicated friend with a perpetual smile on his red, tranquil, weather-beaten face, and a sure aim.

My bedroom was in the loft, next to the area where grain, beans, potatoes and tobacco plants were kept, whilst Pieter and his wife and their nine-year-old daughter Elisabeth slept downstairs. Every morning I would join the little family for a simple but adequate breakfast, after Pieter had prayed in a loud, unnatural voice, followed by a few minutes of silent worship.

In the afternoon Elisabeth came home from school and Pieter returned from the fields. We would all sit down for the main meal of the day of hot potatoes, cabbage, and sometimes a little meat. The dessert was always porridge, and occasionally we had brown beans which had been soaked overnight in vinegar. There was also a peculiar sort of green vegetable which was new to me, called *snijbeet*. After another long extempore prayer Pieter would read a chapter from the Bible. There was no attempt at selection, and the readings began in the first Book of Genesis and continued until we reached the final chapter of the Book of Revelations. I can still remember the last verse of the fifth chapter of St Matthew's Gospel, but for reasons other than religious ones. It was a very long chapter and by the time we reached verse forty-eight '*Weest dan gijlieden volmaakt, gelijk uw Vader, die in de hemelen is, volmaakt is*',* the previously hot meal was ruined.

At about eight o'clock at night, when it was dark, I would go for a short walk through the fields with the good Vrouw, but never into the village, before retiring to bed at nine.

The language of the home was Frisian, but Pieter and Hinke always spoke in Dutch when I was present, so that I could acquire a knowledge of the language which would help me to move to the south of the Netherlands, and also into Flemish-speaking Belgium. The local newspapers were in Dutch with a column or two in Frisian, and the Bible was also in the Dutch language. These were my textbooks.

On reflection, I think it would be difficult for an airman from an English city to adapt himself to the life of a Protestant fundamentalist family in rural Friesland. It was easier for me, as my own background in Pembrokeshire had prepared me to appreciate and understand a bi-lingual rural community united by a powerful and influential church.

All my hosts in Friesland were committed Protestants and members of the Hervormde or the Gereformeerd Church. Sunday was the most important day of the week, and the sermon would be the main topic of conversation. As well as being a religious centre in Garijp, the church was also a social centre, and during the Occupation of great significance to the Resistance movement. The 'Domine' or Minister was an active member of the Resistance, and whenever the Germans were

* Be ye therefore perfect, even as your Father, which is in Heaven, is perfect.

about to make a raid on the village, a warning was often given from the pulpit. Resistance literature and typed summaries of the BBC News were sometimes distributed with the hymn sheets. Pieter came home early from Church one Sunday to say that the Domine had announced before his sermon that he had been given to understand that the German Police were expected to arrive and that any Dutch boys who were in hiding should leave immediately. We had been warned. Pieter also told me that the Germans on a raid would guard the church doors but would never enter the building. The religious freedom of the worshippers was respected as long as they did not pray for their Queen, their country or their Allies. This order was naturally ignored.

The Church had a strong hold over many of the villagers, and the Dijkstra family was no exception. Church members were not expected to play cards, frequent a cinema or a dance hall. I sinned during my early days in Pieter's house as I had been seen shaving on a Sunday morning. I was told that in future I would shave Saturday night in readiness for the Sabbath; even my Welsh Baptist upbringing had not prepared me for this serious reprimand. Vrouw Dijkstra prepared the Sunday lunch the night before, Pieter had his weekly shave, and on Sunday would appear looking quite immaculate in a black suit. He boasted to me that he had never had a bath in his life, but if you saw him on Sunday morning you would never believe it. I was not to be ignored on the Sunday and I was also expected to be properly dressed. Peter gave me one of his black suits, a white shirt and a stiff collar.

Nothing would keep the family away from their Church on Sunday and, when I had surfaced from my cellar on their return, we would have a cup of *surrogaat* coffee which was made from acorns, and then the monthly packet of Consi cigarettes would be passed around. 'Consi' stood for *Cigaretten onder Nationaal Socialistische invloed* – Cigarettes under National Distribution – and were a luxury compared to the home-made cigarettes we smoked during the week. We made our own cigarettes by combining tobacco from the plant next door to my bedroom with filters made of toilet paper. The German-controlled regional newspaper, the *Friesch Dagblad*, was torn into little strips and used for another purpose.

I also associate Sunday with the weekly boiled egg. The only means of heating was the peat-burning stove in the middle of the *voorkamer*, and on Sunday Hinke would place the eggs in a net and place them in the kettle. We would eat our eggs and the same water would be used for making the coffee. We knew how to conserve energy as well as food. My suggestion that perhaps a variation could be introduced into our weekly diet by having a fried egg, '*spiegelei*', was dismissed as being quite unrealistic.

We lived frugally and nothing was wasted. Mealtimes were accompanied by a cacophonous scraping of plates, and on Sunday, when we had meat for dinner, the bones were noisily sucked dry. Pieter also believed that it would be false economy to buy anything which was not of the best material, and on Sunday, and on special occasions, he would discard his '*kiel*' and '*broeken*' and clogs for a high-quality black suit and expensive leather shoes. They were expected to last, and his raincoat was wrapped in brown paper and placed in a cupboard on the last day of March, where it remained until November, irrespective of the weather.

After the prolonged meal, we were allowed to play Dammen – Dutch draughts – and I would watch the ladies pass by our window on their Sunday afternoon parade in their best clothes. Pieter had a cruel sense of humour, and it gave him great delight to describe in detail the most beautiful girl in the village, Famke van der Zee, the baker's daughter, in the full knowledge that his '*onderduiker*' guest would never meet her.

One Sunday Pieter was becoming very agitated, as my courier, Tiny, had not communicated for over a week, and even when she did arrive she did not receive a very warm welcome from Pieter, as he doubted whether she was a regular church-goer and suspected that she used make-up. To make matters worse, she had the audacity to smoke in his company. The main reason, nevertheless, for this cool reception was that she was not of the village but 'of the city'.

A few days later she arrived and presented me with a complete ration book. As a Dutch citizen, I could now draw my full rations, which included in addition to food, a tobacco limit of 40 grammes a fortnight and a packet of cigarette papers, or, as an alternative, twenty Consi cigarettes and twenty grammes of tobacco. The miserable little Consi cigarettes burnt very quickly, but, if I saved my cigarette ends, this amounted to about fifty extra cigarettes a month. My little Oosterwolde pipe was never empty, thanks to the tobacco plant in the loft next to my bedroom.

I tried to make myself as useful as possible about the house. I made my own bed, peeled the potatoes, sliced the beans, made the butter by shaking milk in a bottle, and washed the dishes. I may have even become the best potato peeler in occupied Europe as Vrouw Dijkstra would pick up the peel and, unless she could see a light through it, she would say, '*Te dikke, jongen, veel te dikk*' – too thick, boy, much too thick. By the end of my stay, my potato peelings were thinner than the Consi cigarette paper.

These tasks helped to pass the time and on the whole combined to create quite a relaxing atmosphere. Even so, I had trained myself never to lower my guard completely, and the slightest strange noise would compel me to dive into the cellar. Only a few of the Dijkstras' closest friends and relatives knew of my identity, and I was always forewarned of their visits. One afternoon, when I was busy shelling peas in the loft, an old man in his late eighties barged in without warning. He was Pake, Pieter's father, and he had been informed that I was a Dutch boy from the neighbouring province of Groningen who should be working in Germany. He had no reason to question this statement, and as he was very deaf and my Dutch was improving, the young boy from Groningen and grandfather Dijkstra became very good friends.

During my second week in Garijp a friend of the Dijkstra family came to see me. He was Van der Val, the village butcher, a cool and extremely intelligent man and a member of the Resistance. He became a valued friend and at least once a week

I would visit the butcher's shop late at night and listen to the BBC news on his concealed radio. He had large-scale maps of the battle zones and this self-appointed General would explain in detail military strategy on the various fronts. This was always a great morale-boosting occasion, but equally important was his parting gift of a large wurst sausage. Vrouw Dijkstra would boil the sausage every day for a week to get the fat to put on the potatoes and at the end of the week we would eat the remains. You needed excellent molars to be able to attack the hardened remnants of what was once a perfectly edible sausage.

Van der Val was a good chess player and one day he presented me with a board and a set of chess pieces, but his greatest gift to me was, without doubt, a radio so that I could listen to the news from London. Instead of having to rely on the good news from the church once a week, I was now able to listen to daily news from the BBC. The newly acquired radio was kept in the cellar and I never missed a news bulletin unless visitors came to the house. I was only allowed to listen to the News.

I can remember quite vividly one morning when I was peeling potatoes in the kitchen. Vrouw Dijkstra was listening to the radio in the living room and Pieter was out in the fields. The Germans were having manoeuvres in the village – a realistic effort when hundreds of 'Enemy' prisoners were being marched along the road. Suddenly I saw a young German officer approaching the home. I was able to warn Vrouw Dijkstra and we both managed to dash into the cellar with our precious radio. Vrouw Dijkstra went to speak to the German soldier. I don't know what he asked her but she said that she could not understand him and he went scowling away. After that experience we never switched on the radio unless there was someone on constant guard. By now the Germans had occupied the field adjoining our house, all looking very smart and expertly camouflaged. The roar of an aircraft could be heard in the distance and we debated on whether it was a German or British fighter. We were not left long in doubt as the fighter screamed down and the Germans were scattered in all directions. They did not emerge for quite a while, much to the delight of the Dijkstra family and probably to the entire village.

I was now beginning to get organized and, although I was not able to move to the south, and eventually home, I had now acquired a small circle of loyal friends. One of these was Ruurd Postma, Pieter Dijkstra's nephew from Dokkum, who, like his Uncle Peter, had red hair. He worked in the petroleum office of the *Rijsverkeersinspectie*, the State Traffic Inspection Section, and was in an admirable position to steal coupons for petrol, cigarettes and food for distribution to the Resistance. He used some of the petrol to come to see me on his motor-cycle at least once a fortnight. He was my main contact with the world outside my sheltered little home. He had a good command of English and had an intelligent appraisal of the war situation in general, and of the situation in the Netherlands in particular. He never arrived empty-handed, and in addition to forged coupons he brought an occasional English book, mostly detective stories, and an invaluable English-Dutch dictionary. – the *Campagne's Engelsch Woordenboek*. Although I got to know him very well during my stay in Garijp, and in the post-war years, I was quite unaware until recently of his membership of the KP organization in the Resistance. Even his wife, Alie, had no idea of his involvement until she discovered his authorization papers after his untimely death.

As an employee of the German-controlled State Traffic Inspection Section he was given a permit which allowed him to travel throughout the province and as a member of the KP, a letter from his immediate superior in the Resistance, Piet Oberman (code-named Piet Kramer) enabled him to have the full cooperation of his Resistance colleagues in the pursuit of his underground activities.

It was Ruurd who provided the petrol for the KP operations in Dokkum, and his daughter told me later that he was responsible for the delivery of a car which was used for the attack on the prison in Leeuwarden.

His freedom came to an end on 9 February, 1945. The SD (Sicherheitsdienst – Security Service) rang the front-door bell as he was ready to go to his office in Leeuwarden, and that evening he was sent to prison. He shared a cell with a vicar, a Jew, a Resistance worker and a black-market operator. He was taken to the Burmaniahouse where he appeared before Herr Albrecht and charged with acts of sabotage against the German State. He was very much afraid, as a friend of his, Piet Woudsma, had been shot, and he remembered that he had an English penny in his pocket. He was badly treated by a Herr Grundmann, was found guilty, and returned to his prison cell. In the very early morning of 15 April, 1945, he was released from prison with no explanation given.

Ruurd continued with his Resistance activities and in the last weeks of the Occupation distributed Dutch flags in readiness for the liberation of his native land and victory for a cause to which he was utterly dedicated.

The days, weeks and months passed by with great monotony and even greater frustration. It became quite clear that my only hope of getting home depended on the Allied invasion of Europe. Tiny came to see me one day and said that she had read that three things were necessary to win a war – money, men and time, and then went on to say, 'America has the money, Russia the men and,' after a long pause, 'England the time'.

I still had my maps and in the evenings I would plan a route to Switzerland, Sweden or Spain, but at that time it was impossible to leave the country as all the frontiers were heavily guarded in anticipation of an allied invasion. Only Germans were allowed to go to the coast to the Frisian Islands or to go on the boats to Sweden. My elaborate plans came to nothing. I was desperately anxious to get home, or, failing that, to let my parents know that I was alive.

One day in April a stout, jolly gentleman known to me as 'Dick Mijnheer' arrived at the house with some camera equipment. A fortnight later I was the proud possessor of a genuine Dutch passport which had been stolen from the Town Hall by the Resistance and had once belonged to a man called Arthur Doeke, who had died a few weeks previously. With my new passport, complete with new photograph and fingerprints, I assumed the identity of an "Assistant Accountant' from Den Haag. I memorized the details of my new identity, and got away with it every time.

Resistance fighters never revealed their real names for very obvious reasons, but I discovered later on that 'Dick Mijnheer' was a Minister of Religion in the next village and was known as the 'the shooting padre'. One day a man in RAF uniform had baled out in the early hours of the morning, contacted the Resistance and was interrogated by Dick Mijnheer. The airman spoke German, French, and a few other languages, and claimed that he was an Argentinian flying with the Royal Air Force. The Padre suspected that he was a German sent to spy on the activities of the Resistance. His story may have been true, but the Padre and his colleagues could not take any chances. They shot him.

I knew very little about the organization of the Resistance, but was vaguely aware of the activities of two of the most significant branches operating in Friesland, and probably throughout the Netherlands. One was the Landelijlk Organization, the LO, and the other the Landelijk Knok Ploeg, the KP, of which Ruurd was a member.

The LO was mainly concerned with the administration and maintenance of the 'Onderduikers' the 100,000 or more who spent the war concealed. They were mostly young men who were in hiding because they refused to work for the Germans, but the LO was also responsible for the Jews and the airmen who were 'underground', or to use the name given in Friesland, 'underwater'. It provided food, distributed forged documents, ration cards, and even clothes, and enabled me to have a brand new sports suit and a felt hat for my journey south a few months later, though these articles were almost non-existent in the shops. Kind people were prepared to give up their own clothes and shoes 'for the cause'.

The LO was not primarily concerned with acts of sabotage and this activity was mainly left to the KP.

Rulphink was another active member of the Resistance who

lived in a village about nine kilometres away. He had graduated at the Universities of Leyden and Utrecht and spoke six languages, including Chinese. He had been in the Dutch Foreign Office and it was his intention to go to the Dutch East Indies as a linguist. He had been taken to a concentration camp for refusing to co-operate with the Germans and unwillingly he described to me the conditions in this camp. The internees were mostly Jews and for the first three days no one was given food or clothing. They were ignored rather than punished physically. 'I asked one old lady whether any people died there,' he said, and she answered casually, 'Oh, about four hundred a month.' After six weeks he was asked to sign a statement promising to co-operate with the Germans and give up his studies. He readily agreed, was released and became a member of the Resistance. He had an excellent English library and he gave me books by Scott and Dickens. He had been in hiding since his release.

Spring arrived and brought with it new acquaintances and a new optimism. I could now communicate reasonably well in Dutch, and I was also the proud possessor of a valid passport and a bicycle. I was told that there was an American pilot, Valleau Wilkie, hiding in a farm about two miles away and I decided to visit him. I cycled in broad daylight and had been fully briefed by Pieter as to the exact position of the farm house. Unfortunately the map he drew was not as accurate as it could have been and it was by sheer luck that I did not enter the wrong house. I had walked as far as the door when I noticed two pairs of baby clogs on the step, and as I knew that the farmer and his wife had no children I beat a hasty retreat. My second attempt was successful and, having carefully surveyed the land, I went in to the house and was welcomed by Boer Benedictus and his wife, and Marianna, a Jewish girl who was being hidden by them. I was introduced to Wilkie, the co-pilot of a Flying Fortress bomber who had an interesting story to tell. His plane had been shot up rather badly by a fighter and was rapidly losing height. The First Pilot asked him to take over for a second so that he could check on the crew as the tail gunner had been wounded. When he returned, the plane was down to a minimal altitude of about 2,000 feet, and the order to bale out was given as soon as they knew that the injured crew member could make it.

Valleau and Fred, his Navigator, baled out over Germany, and walked by night into the Netherlands. Valleau was later betrayed in Antwerp and sent to Stalag Luft 3 Prison Camp in Sagan, Lower Silesia.

Marianna had been hiding in the Netherlands for four years. Her family had been sent to Poland and she never heard from them again. She was not very popular in Garijp as her ideas were too modern for the humble Dutch farmer. She had been accustomed to wealth and international travel and had lost everything. Two little nervous, pale and underfed Jewish girls came to see Marianna on the day when I visited her. They had travelled by night from Leeuwarden where they also had been hiding for four years. They had never left the house and the outside world was just a dream, a vision from their bedroom window. They had been invited to spend a week on the farm of the good Boer Benedictus who was sympathetic to the plight of the Jews on religious as well as humanitarian grounds. The Dutch Protestants had a thorough knowledge of the Bible and to persecute the chosen people was a sacrilege in this bastion of Calvinism.

Marianna survived, whereas some 105,000 of the 140,000 Jews who lived in the Netherlands in 1940 died in the gas-chambers and in the concentration camps.

The day before I left Friesland on the first part of the journey to France, Marianna gave me a silk handkerchief with my initials sewn on one corner. She also sewed a name and address into the lining of my new black-market suit. It was her brother's name, the one surviving member of her family who had managed to escape from Germany in time, and was now living in South America. It was an incredibly stupid thing to do as I shall explain later.

In the Netherlands, as in all of the Occupied countries, there were German collaborators in the early years of the war, with the small but articulate Dutch Nazi Party – the NSB – and its armed support, the *Grune Polizei*, keeping a watchful eye on all resistance activities, together with the despised newly-formed organization, the Landwacht, Dutchmen who worked with the Germans for extra pay and double rations. They were not very efficient, but were dangerous as they knew a great deal about their fellow countrymen.

The Dutch people were fully aware of the might of the German forces and their highly successful and short-lived military campaigns. Poland lasted a month, Denmark and Luxemburg a matter of hours, the Netherlands five days, Belgium three weeks and France capitulated in seven weeks. The collaborators were convinced that the war was nearly over and that the Germans were the new masters in Europe, but by 1943 the Resistance was attracting wide support from all sections of the community.

In my village there was only one known active collaborator, and it was decided that he should pay the penalty. He was to be shot. Unfortunately the executioner's aim was inaccurate and the collaborator was only wounded. Nothing happened for three days and then, late one night, the *Grune Polizei* came and knocked at a few doors in the village. The person who answered the door was shot, regardless of age or sex. Three women and four men were shot dead. They knew nothing about the attack on the collaborator. I mention this incident merely to underline the many risks taken by my Resistance friends.

A Thames Television 'World at War' series in 1974 grossly exaggerated the activities of the NSB and prompted a Mr Dekker to write to *The Times* expressing his sadness at this biased presentation. My own letter was in full support and appeared in *The Times* a few days later. It was as follows;

From Dr J. A. Davies.
Sir, Herr Dekker in his letter published on March 16th is certainly not alone in being distressed by the episode on the German occupation of the Netherlands in the Thames Television World at War series. I am sure that his 'profound sense

of sadness and deep disappointment' is shared not only by the Jews and Dutchmen who refused to collaborate with the occupying forces, but by hundreds of British and American airmen who were hidden and helped to survive by the activities of one of the most successful Resistance Movements in occupied Europe.

Whatever may have been the significance of the NSB (National Socialist Party) in the inter-war years, the Dutch people during the German occupation were steadfast in their opposition to Nazism and made incredible sacrifices for the furtherance of the allied cause.

It was my privilege as a member of the RAF to have made contact with the Underground Movement, and to have lived for a short time with Protestant farmers in Friesland and Catholic industrialists in Brabant, all of whom were united in a determined effort to overcome the army of occupation.

I can only attribute the gross distortion in this episode, which exaggerated the importance of the very insignificant NSB and largely ignored the immense patriotism of the Dutch nation and the heroic activities of the Resistance movement, to the producer's reliance on the only documentary material available, which was that issued by the German propaganda machine. The Resistance fighters were 'underground' and not in front of cameras,

I am, Sir, yours faithfully,

J. A. Davies.

In April Ruurd introduced me to another active member of the Resistance, his good friend Jacob H. Boorsma (Jaap) from Dokkum. Jaap and Ruurd had been at school together in Dokkum, and afterwards Jaap attended the Nederlandse School voor Moderne Talen, the Dutch School for Modern Languages in Groningen. During the early years of the war Jaap, together with a few other students, became involved in the production and distribution of the underground magazine *Free Nederlands*, inciting the people to resist the Germans in every way possible and giving information about the Royal Family and other topics which were forbidden by the German authorities. There was an exceptionally active clandestine press, and in addition to the widely read Calvinist *Trouw* and the Communist *De Waarheid*, numerous broadsheets and pamphlets were produced. The *Grune Polizei* were looking for them and they were warned to go into hiding and find a place where the Germans could not find them, as they had been betrayed by a German collaborator.

Jaap was warned that his life was in danger and that he should go into hiding at once. The place chosen was Eernewoude where they had an invaluable Resistance contact in Piet Miedema, the owner of the Hotel Princenhof which became an important Resistance centre. There were many visitors at this picturesque lakeside hotel, and there was a constant demand for young men to work in the hotel and also to go sailing with the visitors in their BM 6-metre boats in the surrounding lakes. It was a good hiding place as the area contained a large number of tourists who were not allowed to go on holidays outside the country and there was a constantly changing population. There was safety in numbers.

Jaap went to live on his own boat for a short time, but this soon became too dangerous and he moved to a safer hiding place in a house in the village of Rinsumageest, and after that to a small houseboat which was hidden in a corner of the Eeltje meer to the west of this village, where he lived during the winter of 1944 and 1945. Rinsumageest was a reasonably safe place as there were no members of the NSB or any other unreliable people in the area.

On 15 May, 1941, all Dutchmen and women over the age of fifteen were forced to carry Identity Cards, with a photograph, fingerprints and personal data, so that the Germans could control the movement of people in the occupied areas and trace young men who were refusing to work as conscripts in German factories. The result was the creation of a major underground industry, the falsification of the information on the Identity Cards. Unless this was done properly the owner of the false document was in great danger. The alterations made on these cards was of paramount importance to the thousands who were in hiding, young men who refused to work in Germany, Jews, and Anglo-American airmen and Resistance fighters.

Andries Heidema carried out this work on behalf of the Jews in Rotterdam until he was discovered and was forced, in February, 1944, to leave and hide in Rinsumageest in Friesland, where he carried on this highly dangerous job in a small attic in the shop of Foeke de Jong. In 1944 Jaap, who was also in hiding in the area, joined him. They made the attic smaller by constructing a temporary wall to conceal their workshop, where they had batteries, chargers and all the equipment necessary to carry out this highly intricate work. With Aceton, glue, small tweezers and a powerful magnifying glass they made alterations even to the photographs. Sometimes they could only complete two Identity Cards in one night, although they had a few hundred to modify. This work went on quietly and the shop-owner was not aware of what was going on. Although they did not use much electricity, they worked mostly at night and the increased consumption showed on the meter. This was discovered by the Electricity Board inspectors, but, as they were more than sympathetic to the Resistance, the meter was replaced by a new one and no further action was taken. The Germans once made a search but they were unable to find the hiding place. About 200 Identity Cards had been changed and these were distributed by reliable civil servants.

The winter of 1944 was cold and, though we were eating reasonably well in Friesland, there was a serious food shortage in the cities in the west of the Netherlands. The butcher, Lutzer van der Wal, was fully occupied in Kornelis F. Boersma's farmhouse and a considerable amount of meat was produced for illegal distribution. The ear tags of the cattle were changed so often that the German administration system broke down completely and they had no idea as to what was happening to the cattle. The butchers were kept busy and they also deserve an honourable mention in the Resistance struggle. The problems of distribution were overcome as the meat was transported to the water tower in Leeuwarden in a barge belonging to the 'Fresh Water Supply Company'. The Company's workers had all their equipment on the deck to give the impression that they were about to go on a major repair operation. They would come close to a farmhouse on a small canal, and at night the meat was brought to a lorry and stowed away. At one stage there was a fortnightly transportation of meat. My good friend Jaap, with his colleague, Sake de Walle, brought some meat in a rowing boat at night as far as Dokkum, until one night the Dutch Quisling organizations, the Landwacht, found out what was happening. Jaap and his fellow workers in the Resistance were not taken to prison, but their activity came to an end and the meat, together with the bicycles and other possessions, were confiscated.

One day Ruurd came to the Eernewoude district with coupons which he had stolen for the Resistance and visited his old school friend Jaap, but with a specific request. He said that he knew of three airmen, two RAF and one American, who had been hidden for quite a time under difficult circumstances and without any opportunity to live a natural life in the open air. He asked Jaap whether it would be possible for them to have a few days' sailing on the peaceful and relatively safe waters of the great lakes. Jaap agreed immediately and this adventurous plan was put into operation.

It was now the month of May and a temporary taste of freedom. We had been tipped off that the Germans were about to launch a raid on the village and this was the excuse given to accept an invitation to join Ruurd and his friend Jaap on what they termed a 'sailing holiday'. I cycled to the farm of our friend Boer Kleusterman, about four miles away, where they were both waiting for me in a small boat and we rowed along the canal until we came to Jaap's boat on the lake. It was comfortably furnished and that evening we listened to the one and only English record on a gramophone over and over again. It was called 'Good Night Sweetheart' and the risk was well worth taking with only the clear sky and the wide expanse of water as a witness.

We sailed the next day from Eernewoude towards the lakeside village of Grouw and then on to Mooidamen, with the confidence of properly dressed sailors wearing the traditional cap. It was so very peaceful on the picturesque Lake Princenhof. We were among a labyrinth of deep silent pools fringed with waving reeds, where water birds made their nests. Rest and tranquillity ruled and we were alone with nature in all its serenity.

We were brought back to reality a few hours later when we moored at the side of a restaurant called Isicht and sat on the terrace sipping our coffee. After about half an hour a big motor boat moored next to us and three young men about our age got out, sat at the next table and ordered drinks. They put on their jackets and we could see that they were German officers. This was a very bad moment and we all realized the danger we were in. Nobody spoke. I went to the toilet and when I returned Jaap and Ruurd had paid the bill and we walked very slowly to our own boat. Jaap was in a bath of perspiration, but we sailed away without arousing any suspicion. As it happens there were no real problems, as we were told later that they were German airmen who were not looking for evaders, but were only there for a few days' leave from flying duties. Nevertheless it was an anxious half hour and I thought that we had all put on a good act.

There was a flourishing 'Black Market' at the Hotel Princenhof and the owner, Piet Miedema, worked closely with the aircrew survivors, and was fully aware of our 'holiday'. On one occasion an American Flying Fortress crash-landed near the hotel. Piet and Jaap spirited two of the survivors to the home of Wilt Kooistra, a sail-maker in the nearby village of Oudega who was prepared to hide them. The others are buried in the village of Eernewoude.

Jaap's father-in-law was also hiding in a farmhouse in Rinsumageest. The Dutch Government in exile in 1944 called for a railway strike which brought the Dutch railways to a standstill and, as an engineer on the Dokkum train, he obeyed the call and went into hiding. Many of these strikers stayed out and the Resistance supplied the railwaymen with strike pay through a network of messengers on bicycles, mostly young girls.

I lived in comparative luxury during these three days; we

even had fried eggs for breakfast. In the evenings the only sounds which could be heard on this tranquil lake were the occupants of the other boats singing vigorously the Dutch National Anthem, Wilhelmus van Nassauwe, and national folk songs. The occasional German Patrol Boat was the only reminder that we were in an occupied land and that our freedom was only temporary.

I returned to Garijp at the end of the third day. This was most fortunate as the boat was raided by the Landwacht the following evening. These collaborators had been informed that a young evader was being hidden there, but they were seen approaching the boat and the boy jumped into the lake and escaped.

The 'holiday' was over but there was one other visit to Eernewoude. The Resistance had their own barber and in those days the writer of these memoirs had a considerable amount of hair. My daughters do not believe it. The barber was Rinse Postma and he came to our house in Garijp about once a month. He was a splendid man and convinced me that it would be perfectly safe to visit him in Eernewoude. No one would know that I was not Arthur Doeke but James Arthur Davies. I cycled in fine spirits and met Rinse on the outskirts of the village. He took me to his home and introduced me to the eight members of his family, who were all aware that I was a British airman.

Behind the house a motor boat was waiting to take me to a yacht moored further up the lake. A gentleman appeared and said in English, 'How do you do, Sir? All airmen are friends of mine'. He was a Captain in the Dutch Army and was hiding in a little thatched cottage on one of the lake's small islands. A member of the Royal Air Force from Newfoundland had been staying with him on the island but had been caught. By now there was tight security in and around Eernewoude and this was to be my last visit before leaving the province. As I boarded the motor boat, the owner turned to me and said '*Veel beter dan in gevangenis, niet waar?*' (Much better than being in a prison camp, isn't it?)

The interval between these two expeditions had been a very

dull one with the same routine every day, the same hopes, the same frustrations, the same failures.

There were only about five occasions during my long stay in Garijp when I was able to leave my sheltered home and cycle in broad daylight with Pieter to open fields about five kilometres away. Keeping away from the villages and looking very much the Dutch peasant in my wooden clogs, black trousers and blue 'kiel', I acknowledged the greetings of the passers-by until we reached a secluded resting place near a small canal. There was an uncanny stillness, and the usually excitable, tense and volatile Pieter suddenly became a changed person. He was now at peace with his Maker, and at this mystical moment there was an extra greenness to the grass under the cloudless sky and the uninterrupted wide horizons. He looked towards the heavens, and in a quiet, gentle and natural voice said, over and over again, 'Vrede, jongen, Vrede' (Peace, my boy, Peace) and then the words of the Psalmist: 'Hij doet mij nederliggen in grazige weiden; Hij voert mij zachtkens aan zeer stille wateren' (He maketh me to lie down in green pastures: he leadeth me beside the still waters).

We cycled back, very slowly, to the claustrophobic confines of my partitioned bedroom next to the grain, beans, and potatoes and tobacco plants.

There was one other visit to the outside world when I was able to accompany my good friend the butcher, Van der Val, on a fishing expedition in the local canal.

The boredom was punctuated by a game of Dammen in the evenings, but the main morale booster was listening to the European Service of the BBC. I would hang on to every item of news, speculating on when the invasion of Europe would take place.

One day the Germans were having manoeuvres in the field next to our house, when an RAF fighter plane dived down and machine-gunned them – much to our immense satisfaction and their embarrassment. A few weeks later an American Liberator crashed into a nearby windmill in the late afternoon, killing all the crew.

Birthdays in the Netherlands are significant events, and little calendars of birthdays could be seen in most houses. Tante

Trien, Pieter's sister and my worthy adopted aunt, celebrated her birthday with us. We were all in our Sunday-best clothes, and having offered our warmest congratulations, drank endless cups of *surrogaat* coffee, and ate precious pieces of chocolate and the traditional cake. Little Elisabeth's contribution to the party was her rendering of a song which I had taught her to sing in English, 'I've got sixpence'.

There was another birthday which caused me a great deal of anxiety at the time. The good Vrouw Dijkstra had gone into the village, Pieter to the fields and Elisabeth to school. I was on my own in the kitchen when an aggressive looking woman burst in without knocking and greeted me in a loud voice with the words, *'Mynheer, vandaag is de verjaardag van de Führer* (Today is Hitler's birthday). She sat down and for nearly an hour I was forced to listen to this unwelcome guest. Fortunately she was prepared to do all the talking, and all I had to do was to break in occasionally with a 'yes', a 'no' or a 'perhaps', and give the impression that we were on the same wave-length. Vrouw Dijkstra eventually arrived, the exhausting monologue ended and, as I crept upstairs, I overheard my unexpected guest saying, 'What a nice boy you have staying with you from Den Haag, but isn't he very quiet.'

This is the only reason why I still remember Hitler's birthday on the 20th of April.

I read anything I could find during this tense period of waiting for something to happen, including the local paper, the German-controlled *Friese Courant*, but did not accept the invitation in a full-page advertisement to become a volunteer in the German Navy, *'Vrijwilligers voor de Kriegsmarine'*.

'ENGELSCH TROEPEN IN FRANKRIJK' (English troops are in France). With these stupendous words Pieter dashed into my bedroom on that memorable morning of the 6th of June, 1944. I shouted *'Invasie*? Invasion?' but Pieter shook his head and said, *'Nein*, but there are some English troops in France,' and with these words the greatest amphibious operation ever mounted in the whole history of warfare was dismissed.

75

I dashed downstairs, switched on the radio in the cellar and the invasion of Europe was confirmed. Pieter was now convinced that the invasion had at last taken place and anticipated an immediate increase in his tobacco ration, and an end to the German occupation of his native land. The village of Garijp came to life and we all expected an early end to the war in Europe. This was my long-awaited opportunity to leave for home. There was now no excuse.

The European war went on for another year.

The German-controlled newspapers announced in bold headlines that the Germans had brought into operation a new secret weapon which would overcome their temporary reversals – a pilotless plane known as the V1. Where conventional arms were failing, money and manpower was poured in for these new weapons, the V originally standing for 'Versuchmuster' (experimental type), but later in order to improve morale in the bombed cities, the German propaganda machine declared that it meant 'Vergeltungswaffen', a weapon of revenge. Page after page was dedicated to this diversionary propaganda, but it was not taken seriously in Friesland. Only after my return home did I have any idea of the destructive power of the V1 and V2 missiles. The Germans were convinced that this new weapon could turn the tide in their favour and that they possessed even deadlier missiles which would be launched within the next few months. My Dutch friends smiled, and one of them said, 'The V1 is a flying machine without a pilot, the V2 a pilot without a flying machine, the V3 a huge German tank with eighty men, one inside and 79 pushing it.' He then referred to the technical superiority of the Ford V8 motor car and dismissed the German V threat as being of no consequence.

My friends in the Resistance had a peculiar but refreshing sense of humour, a quality which cost one Dutch comedian his freedom. There was a public concert in Leeuwarden and a large number of German officers and men were present. The comedian went on to the stage, raised his right hand in a Nazi salute and the German soldiers stood to attention and acknowledged the salute with 'Heil Hitler', then sat down. The comedian kept his hand raised and added, 'The snow was so high in Friesland in 1928'. He was arrested.

Pieter recalled with immense pleasure the day when a German officer went to the hairdresser in Leeuwarden to have a haircut and a shave. The barber slit his throat.

After a month of stubborn fighting in the Caen area, there was a dramatic military breakthrough, and from then on, after a long period of stagnation, events moved very quickly.

The Domine, Dick Mijnheer, and one of the leaders of the Resistance in the north came to see me and asked me whether I would now like to try to get home through the south of the Netherlands, Belgium and France. They made it quite clear that if captured I would probably be shot, as I would be in civilian clothes and had been in the country for many months with a forged passport. I was quite confident that I could make it.

There was a farewell party the night before I left, when the few friends who had helped me during this unnatural and rather tense period came to wish me well on my journey to the south. Pieter sat in his usual place at the head of the table in his Sunday suit, the good Vrouw, benign as ever, provided us with a splendid feast in spite of the shortages, and little Elisabeth wore her best frock and a new string of beads. The guests at this never-to-be-forgotten party were the jovial Tante Trien, the fearless Jopie of the Resistance, Mr and Mrs Van der Val, Boer Benedictus, Boer Kleusterman, Rinse the barber and Bill Deknatel. It had been a long period of inactivity and frustrated hopes, time which was measured not in months or weeks but in days. To be exact, 124 long days and nights.

It was 5.30 the following morning when Pieter woke me, and with my adopted family we cycled for a few kilometres to get a tram to Leeuwarden. The butcher and his wife were at their window, and so was Tante, to wave goodbye. It was an emotional parting. Vrouw Dijkstra unashamedly wept and Pieter's firm handshake symbolized a bond of friendship and understanding which was to last until his death at the age of sixty-eight. The last words were from the very old young Elisabeth who told me to be very careful.

CHAPTER FIVE

SOUTH TO BRABANT

I arrived in Leeuwarden, the busy provincial capital, on a market day and, with a tremendous feeling of exhilaration, mingled with the farmers for nearly an hour before meeting 'Andere Mijnheer'. He had already bought me a first class railway ticket as I was no longer a Dutch peasant in a blue smock, black trousers and clogs, but a young man expensively attired in a blue sports suit, felt hat and new shoes. I was told that it was safer to travel first class as there were frequent inspections in the other class for black market operators and other illegal passengers! I bought a newspaper and, properly dressed, melted like a chameleon into the ambience of a first-class compartment of respectable citizens and German officers.

There was no sign of Tiny at the station, but I now understand that she had been in touch with her contact, a Mr R. Vermeulen, from Drachten, who was himself hiding in Leeuwarden, and was the contact man for the international organization for assisting airmen to return to the United Kingdom. After so many frustrating delays, Tiny had been informed that at last it was reasonably safe for me to go 'down the line'. The 'line' was the long and dangerous journey, which was divided into sectors, each sector having a different guide. Although the 'line' often broke, and some guides were arrested, the 'All clear' was given for a successful journey home through the south of the Netherlands, Belgium and France.

The guides were usually changed on the platforms of the railway stations and, as one guide did not know the identity of the next, they had to wear a special identification, in Tiny's case a very ugly hat of a venomous green colour.

We had to change trains at Arnhem, and it was at this station that I saw Tiny for the first time since we had met in Garijp many weeks previously. I was quite unaware that she was on the same train. I would have loved to have greeted her, but had to ignore her completely and show no sign of recognition. She could have been condemned to death.

I followed her at some distance, saw her shake hands and talk to a man for a few seconds, and without as much as a glance or a wink, she took the next train back to Leeuwarden. Her task had been completed, and I did not see her again until she came to stay with my parents in Wales shortly after the end of the war in Europe.

For the first part of the journey, Andere Mijnheer, a young girl from the Resistance, and I had the good fortune of having a compartment to ourselves, but at the next station two men entered. Nobody spoke and I read my newspaper in peace.

On this glorious sunny day our peaceful journey was suddenly interrupted, as our colleagues in RAF Fighter Command took full advantage of the cloudless conditions and decided to try to put our railway engine out of action. There was an abrupt halt, as the air-raid warning had been sounded, and I noticed a yellow flag hanging from the signal box indicating the presence of allied aircraft. The German light Ack-Ack men were soon in action from a special carriage which was attached to the train. There was some delay but we eventually arrived at Zwolle.

We left the station and followed 'Andere Mijnheer' to a field on the outskirts of the town. I was slightly disturbed to see that we were being followed by two men, but there was no cause for alarm, as our guide introduced them to me later as American airmen who had recently been shot down. We all enjoyed lunch together in this open field, and after an hour or two returned to the station to continue our journey. The Americans and I decided to part company for security reasons and to meet later in Arnhem.

The journey was uneventful and I shared the compartment with a German officer who very politely asked me to open the window, and then offered me a cigarette. I opened the window but refused his generous offer. There was no further conversation and the train pulled into Arnhem where I was to meet two blonde ladies of the Resistance.

As a result of the acute paper shortage, the Railway officials often issued one ticket to be shared between two or three people travelling in the same direction and at the same time. One of the American airmen had our ticket, but, as soon as he saw the women, he dashed out into the street through the barrier, leaving two of us without a ticket. Luckily his fellow American acted very quickly and, as we approached the gate, he pointed to me, and I did the same to the unfortunate person next in the line. The ticket collector shouted, but there was a large crowd at the barrier and we were able to push our way through to join the others who were anxiously waiting for us. That was a bad moment.

We all went to a small hotel where we had something to eat, and then walked with the two girls into one of the municipal parks. They were both medical students at Utrecht and had been active in the Resistance for two years. They left us on our own for an hour so that they could check the train times and buy our tickets. I met them later outside the station, but on my way there I was pushed off the pavement by two arrogant young men wearing large Swastika arm-bands. They were members of the Hitler Youth Movement, '*Hitlerjugend*', and would probably have made a name for themselves had they discovered the identity of the man in the blue suit.

We left our two guides at the station and caught the Nijmegen train. It was very crowded and unfortunately I had to stand in the corridor next to a Dutch nurse who was anxious to talk. First she asked me the time and, having given her this information, she wanted to know why the Arnhem train was so late, and when did I think we would arrive. I was saved by another passenger who was able to give her the answers. I went to the toilet and when I returned I stood next to a Japanese gentleman with the Rising Sun emblem on his tunic.

A number of passengers got off at the next stop, and the two Americans and I had a seat in the same compartment, together with two young girls from the Resistance. They had been given our photographs in advance, with detailed personal descriptions, so that there could be no chance of making a mistake. They entered at the same time as a young man, exchanged friendly greetings and placed their bags together on the rack and sat down in the corner farthest away from us. The man took out an English novel from his briefcase, smiled amiably at us, made a few remarks about the weather, and I assumed that he was also a member of the Resistance. I nevertheless decided to keep quiet and read my Dutch newspaper.

We had to change trains once again, and had to wait a long time for our connection. I never saw the young man again, and later the two girls told me that they had met him for the first time at the station, and as far as they knew he had nothing to do with the Resistance. We could so easily have spoken and probably endangered the lives of our two guides.

We soon arrived in Nijmegen where I had been given the address of a reliable contact, and two days later travelled by train and bicycle to the village of Sprang where I met Piet Felix, an active Resistance worker who had the responsibility of taking me to stay with my final contact in the Netherlands. Piet was a member of 'André', the vitally important Resistance group in Brabant which had been responsible for the transportation of about one hundred and eighty refugees and evaders between 1940 and 1945. They came mostly from the Netherlands and Germany and included a large number of Jews.

Piet Felix had enlisted in the Dutch Army in January, 1940. Five months later the Germans occupied the Netherlands and he was discharged as he had found employment in a large steel factory in Utrecht. He soon resigned, and in a subtle way demonstrated his opposition to the German invaders by casting thousands of Dutch military helmets in plaster, depicting a lion with the seven Dutch provinces held firmly in its claws. The helmet was painted in red, white and blue, the colours of the Dutch flag, and in orange, the colour of the Royal family. In April, 1943, he was forced to go 'underground' as all ex-servicemen were commanded to report to the occupying powers. He refused to obey and was hidden in Kaatsheuvel where there was an active Resistance movement. Piet was critical of the way in which the Dutch Resistance was organized in the early years of the Occupation, with many individual acts of resistance and sabotage operating in isolation, but by the beginning of 1943 a well co-ordinated movement gradually emerged. On his arrival in Kaatsheuvel he contacted the resistance group 'André', who provided him with forged food ration cards, and who later involved him in their activities. His first task was to distribute forged ration cards to those who were hiding in the district and also to circulate illegal Resistance bulletins. There was a powerful German military presence in Kaatsheuvel at this time which made his next assignment particularly dangerous – escorting hidden Jews by bicycle from Sprang to safer hiding places in Den Bosch on the first part of their journey to freedom.

From the beginning of 1944 he became actively involved in an activity known as 'Pilot help' within Group 'André', giving assistance to allied airmen who had baled out or crash landed over enemy territory.

The activities of the Resistance were curtailed by the very strict curfew regulations imposed by the Germans, which operated in Brabant from 8 o'clock in the evening until 5 in the morning. One was liable to be shot if one was still outside during curfew. There was one occasion, when half an hour before curfew, Piet received a message asking him to pick up a crate of light bulbs. The 'light bulbs' were three shot-down airmen and he met them at the designated place where they were ready for him on their bicycles. There was a sense of urgency as darkness had already begun to fall and they had to go to Kaatsheuvel as quickly as possible. Piet cycled in front of the three airmen, checking from time to time to see whether they were still following him. It was now nearly eight o'clock and the cycling was fast and furious in order to be home in time for curfew. Many other cyclists were similarly motivated and were cycling in the same direction, but when Piet looked backwards to make a final check he noticed that the airmen were following a total stranger. He managed to get to a telephone and told a Resistance colleague that he had lost 'the crate of light bulbs'. They were found, but by this time it was pitch dark and any light was forbidden as the black-out regulations were rigorously imposed. It was far too risky to continue on their journey to Kaatsheuvel so they had to go back to Sprang.

Piet experienced moments of elation as well as moments of near panic. He once took six airmen to a safe house in the centre of Kaatsheuvel on a busy market day when there was a fair in full swing. The little town was crowded and the fair was held in the market square directly in front of the house. They entered without any problem and sat down in the living room which was on the street side and played a game of cards. It soon became very crowded outside with visitors and off-duty German soldiers enjoying all the fun of the fair. Suddenly a noisy group of German soldiers approached, sat on the window sill, greeted the card players, drank large quantities of local beer, and left the nervous players in peace to concentrate on their game, and Piet with a feeling of victory.

A week later Piet tried to help the airmen to reach the Belgian border. They had already been given bicycles, but, as it was twelve noon, the sirens were sounded for the lunch break with the result that the streets became crowded with Germans as well as the local workers. Piet was already on his cycle but discovered to his alarm that the airmen had never ridden a bicycle, and in his words, 'Like dead drunk men they were wandering about and I was afraid that they might fall and would then receive help from passers-by, and perhaps they would start to use their own language. I decided that we should walk wheeling our bikes with good pace.'

Piet did not know my name or the name of his contact. I was merely number 25 and he was instructed to meet me at the village of Sprang before continuing by bicycle to Horst 7 in Kaatsheuvel, the home of Simon and Dina de Cock.

Simon and Dina de Cock and their four young children lived in a delightful villa in its own grounds outside the village of

Kaatsheuvel near Tilburg. At the time of my visit the eldest child, Mien, was aged seven, Mieke six, Greet five, and Wim three. I was introduced to Simon and Dina by Piet Felix, but not by name.

Simon was an avid naturalist and was an authority on the migration of birds, and it was the intention at one time to publish his detailed notes and diagrams. He had an impressive library and read one French and one English novel every week. Before the war he had travelled extensively in Europe and North America and was a man of very wide culture. He was also an enthusiastic and competent artist, and on my second day in his home, when I greeted him by his correct name, he was very alarmed and demanded to know the name of the person who had disclosed it. He had already told me of his interest in painting, and all I had to do was to point to the six pictures on the walls of his living room. He had forgotten to erase the name of the artist – S. de Cock.

The contrast between my life with Pieter Dijkstra in Friesland and Simon de Cock in Brabant could not have been greater. The two men were products of different cultural, social and religious environments, but they were united in their determination to do everything possible to get rid of the common enemy.

Vrouw de Cock, like Vrouw Tiesinga and Vrouw Dijkstra, was a brave, kind and determined lady who received me with great kindness and generosity, and who fully supported her husband's Resistance activities during a period of intense danger.

I spent most of the time hiding on the flat roof of their villa, where their one trustworthy maid would bring me food. Sometimes I was allowed into the library, but for most of the time I had to remain behind locked doors. I was not only hiding from visitors, but also from the young de Cock children who were unaware of my presence. One morning, however, Mieke came unexpectedly home from school and I had forgotten to lock the bathroom door. The little girl walked in, saw me, and dashed downstairs shouting 'Daddy, Daddy, there is a man in the bath with big eyes'. Her father had to make up a story and

19. American PoWs working a blower (*see diagram p 136*).

20. Stalag 3A Luckenwolde. PoWs walking the perimeter.

1	2	3	4	5	6	7	8	9	10	11	12	13	14	15	16	1̶			21	22	2̶		25

Personalkarte I: Personelle Angaben (Tr.Nr. 30)

Beschriftung der Erkennungsmarke:
Nr. 698

Kriegsgefangenen-Stammlager: *James Arthur*   Lager: Kgf.Lag.d.Lw.7

Name: D A V I E S

Vorname: James Arthur

Geburtstag und -ort: 12.1.23, B... ...-
...hire

Religion: ...C...

Vorname des Vaters:

Familienname der Mutter:

Staatsangehörigkeit: England

Dienstgrad: Sgt.

Truppenteil: RAF.   Komp. usw.: A/G

Zivilberuf: Student   Berufs-Gr.:

Matrikel Nr. (Stammrolle des Heimatstaates): 1.651 8

Gefangennahme (Ort und Datum): 1o.8.44, Grön...

Ob gesund, krank, verwundet eingeliefert:

Lichtbild		Nähere Personalbeschreibung	
	Größe / **Haarfarbe**	**Besondere Kennzeichen:**	
	1,68 / braun		

Fingerabdruck des rechten (!) Zeigefingers

Name und Anschrift der zu benachrichtigenden Person in der Heimat des Kriegsgefangenen

Mr. Davies

Bryn Hedydd Bonacath
Pembrokeshire Wales

689   DAVIES, J.A.   Wenden!

Personal-Beschreibung:

Figur:	mittekräftig
Größe:	1,68
Alter:	21 J.
Gesichtsform:	oval
Gesichtsfarbe:	gesund
Schädelform:	rund
Augen:	blau
Nase:	breit
Haare:	braun
Bart:	--
Gebiß:	gesund, 1 Schneidezhn fehlt
Besondere Merkmale:	--
Deutsche Sprachkenntnisse:	--
Gewicht:	68 kg

Bemerkungen:

Name: Lager: Idschtlung der Erkennungsmarke Nr.

21 & 22. Author's Prisoner of War Identity Cards.

Dulag-Luft. **Kriegsgefangenenkartei.**

Gefangenen-Erkennungsmarke	Dulag-Luft Eingeliefert
Nr. 688	am: 26.8.44 L.

NAME: **D A V I E S**

Vornamen: **James Arthur**

Dienstgrad: **Sgt.** Funktion: **A/G.**

Matrikel-No.: **1 651 898**

Geburtstag: **12.1.23**

Geburtsort: **Boncath Pembrokeshire**

Religion: **baptist**

Zivilberuf: **Student**

Staatsangehörigkeit: **britisch**

Vorname des Vaters:

Familienname der Mutter:

Verheiratet mit:

Anzahl der Kinder:

Heimatanschrift:
Mr. Davies
Bryn Hedydd
Boncath
Pembrokeshire Wales

Abschuß am: **19.2.44** bei: **Groningen** Flugzeugtyp: **Lanc.**

Gefangennahme am: **10.8.44** bei: **W.O.**

Nähere Personalbeschreibung

Statur: **mittel kräftig**

Größe: **168 cm**

Schädelform: **rund**

Haare: **braun**

Gewicht: **68 kg**

Gesichtsform: **oval**

Gesichtsfarbe: **gesund**

Augen: **blau** (34)

Nase: **breit**

Bart:

Gebiß: **gesund**
1 Schneidez. gebr.

Besondere Kennzeichen:

Front Profil Fingerabdruck (Rechter Zeigefinger)

23. The daily food ration. The bucket holds soup for over 200 prisoners.

24. Our Russian 'liberators' who kept us for six weeks as pawns in a political game.

said that somebody had fallen in the street and was very dirty and had asked permission to use the bathroom.

The war between Simon and the German Reich started soon after the Occupation because his main hobby had been threatened, the flying of his valuable long-distance racing pigeons. The German authorities had issued an order that pigeons would have to be kept under cover, as they could be used for spying. Simon's pigeon loft could hardly be seen as his extensive garden was surrounded by high trees, so he ignored the order and let them fly as usual. This continued for a few weeks, but one day when he came home he saw a young German officer shooting at them as they were flying. Simon told him to stop immediately and that he would call them in. The officer told him that they would be confiscated and took them with him. In Simon's words, 'I then had a hot discussion telephonically with the German Commander,' who ordered him to come to Den Bosch the following morning. His plea that his pigeons were his only hobby and that they were very dear to him was of no avail, and he lost his birds. He was warned that as he had breached a serious order, any further disobedience would mean the concentration camp. He was released, but was now more determined than ever to oppose the Germans in every way possible. He loved his pigeons. This was now a very personal war.

Simon owned a blanket factory in Tilburg and when the Germans invaded his country he was ordered to hand over his products to the occupying forces. In 1942 a well-intentioned friend came to see him to say that he had a large quantity of wool which he had never disclosed to the Germans and asked Simon whether he was prepared to make blankets for the Resistance. He discussed the proposition with his business partner and readily agreed as the circumstances were favourable at the time. There were very few German soldiers in Tilburg as they were nearly all on the various fighting fronts, and the factory was empty. Simon was still sore after the pigeon affair, and the blankets were produced for many months until the end of 1942.

All went well until a few days before Christmas, when a

business friend from Amsterdam came to warn him that the German Military Police had found out about the forbidden blanket production. Unfortunately it was too late as the wool was already in the machines and could not be taken away in time. On the next day, when Simon was having his lunch in his office, two men with drawn revolvers came in and he was immediately arrested. They were Quislings, Dutch people who were collaborating with the Germans. They went to the factory and saw the incriminating evidence. They then went to his partner's home in the same street and they were both taken to the Police Station where they spent the night sleeping on wooden planks. The next morning they were taken to the Head Office of the German SS in The Hague.

The Police in Tilburg were all anti-German and informed Dina and his partner's wife that they had been taken away. Simon and his partner were handcuffed and marched to the railway station, and were about to enter the compartment when they heard their wives shouting 'Simon and Jan'. The railway guard was about to give the command to start but waited for a few minutes so that their wives could speak to them before returning to their homes.

In The Hague they were taken in a prison van to the SS prison where they had to wait for two hours in a small room beside the main entrance. This brief stay made a lasting impression on Simon when he saw for the first time the treatment which some of his fellow countrymen received. On two occasions he witnessed Dutch prisoners being beaten with sticks until they fell bleeding to the ground.

After two hours a German officer took Jan to an office to be interrogated, while Simon had to wait outside for another hour before being called. He vividly remembers being placed in front of a powerful searchlight and could vaguely see a little group of German officers. As his name was Simon he was very much afraid that he would be accused of being a Jew, but after an hour's examination, it was all over, and he returned to the small waiting room. Four hours later the same officer who had interrogated him came in and made a long speech about the serious consequences of contravening the German law, and that, if it happened again, he would certainly be taken to a concentration camp. He then went on to say that as the prisons were full, and as it was a few days before Christmas, they could go home. Simon was convinced that he had witnessed a miracle. He arrived home at midnight.

The 'well-intentioned' friend who came to see him in 1942 made another visit shortly after Christmas and said that he still had a quantity of wool, and once again Simon and his partner Jan decided, in spite of previous warnings, to continue with the distribution of blankets. This went on for another few months, until the SS arrested Jan. Simon received a telephone call from Jan's daughter to tell him what had happened, and he immediately went into hiding. He slept in different places, avoided arrest, and eventually was able to return to his own home. He became very depressed and had the greatest difficulty in living with the knowledge that he was free but Jan had been captured.

The second 'miracle' was about to take place. Jan had been friendly for many years with a German family who now had a son who was a high-ranking officer in the Army, and who had recently been posted to Holland. He went to visit Jan and his family and, when he heard what had happened, he took immediate action. Within a week Jan was freed.

Kaatsheuvel is close to the River Rhine and Simon and Dina were fully aware of the drama which was being enacted in the skies above them as the Allied aircraft made their deadly journeys to the Ruhr, and were deeply moved by the sight of many crippled and burning bombers. Many of the airmen who succeeded in baling out at night landed on farm lands, and it was a question of luck whether they were picked up by the Germans or made contact with the Resistance. They were often brought by a farmer to a priest or a doctor, and from then they would be handed over to members of the Underground movement.

One day in 1942 Simon's family doctor, who was a member of the Resistance, came to see him, said that he was in deep trouble and asked for help. Two American airmen had been shot down during the night and would have to be hidden for a few days until it was safe for them to be taken by Piet Felix to the Belgian frontier. After a brief consultation with his wife, Simon readily agreed, and that was the beginning of his involvement with air-crew escapers.

Two weeks later the doctor came with another demand: a hiding place was required for two Canadian airmen and a 'Brazilian'. Simon agreed at once, but the next day the doctor called again with unexpected news which heralded a short period of great tension and suspense. The 'Brazilian' was a German officer. Simon and Dina were now in great danger. The doctor gave Simon a revolver with the command that if the 'Brazilian' attempted to escape he should be shot. The revolver was placed between the books in the book-case in the children's room. The Brazilian's name was Joe Heims and he stayed with Simon and Dina until the liberation of the Netherlands.

This was his story. His father was a German Consul in one of the big cities in Brazil, his parents had been divorced and his mother returned to Germany. With the rapidly deteriorating political situation in Europe, he decided to visit his mother, and war was declared. He made every attempt to return to Brazil, but it was too late. He was a German citizen and was compelled to do his military service. As an engineer and speaking four languages he was immediately commissioned in the German Army. He waited for an opportune moment in which to escape, and eventually made contact with a Resistance sympathizer and entered the aircrew escape line. Simon believed him, and he became a good friend. One of the Canadian airmen wanted to shoot him on the spot but Simon's judgement was correct, and Joe Heims became a valuable ally as well as a friend in the traumatic days which lay ahead. This highly competent engineer was largely responsible for the underground shelter in the front garden and for the secret exit from the house.

There was not much room for this large family and there was always a fight as to who was to sleep next to little Wim. With a quiet efficiency, Dina controlled this extended household. She was very inventive and when her eldest daughter,

Mien, saw an airman in the bedroom she was told that he was a painter and decorator and had come to see what paper and colour was required. The children were given the impression that it was perfectly normal to have a number of visitors in the house.

In October, 1944, the Allied forces were approaching the Belgian border, not far from Tilburg, and, as Dina was six and a half months pregnant, her doctor said that she would have to go to hospital in Tilburg. She proudly refused to go in a German Red Cross ambulance, but no one would risk driving a car as RAF fighter planes attacked every vehicle on the roads. With the help of an underground friend, Simon and the pregnant Dina cycled the 15 kilometres to Tilburg, Dina on the back of the cycle. They left the bicycle in the home of a former neighbour at the entrance of the town and walked to the hospital. The doctor did not have the time for a full investigation but realized that there was something wrong and she was immediately admitted. Simon had to return because of the danger but when he arrived his servant and children were crying as there had been a major air attack on the village and Wim was missing. The scared little three-year-old had run across the street to a nearby cafe and fortunately the owner, who had been a maid at his home, recognized him and brought him back when there was a lull in the fighting.

Two days later it was war with a vengeance. Dina was in hospital on the night when Tilburg was liberated. The bombardment had been intense but the nurse forgot to place a bell near her bed. After a while she heard somebody shouting, 'Have they all gone to the shelters?' and there was a moment of panic. She picked up every movable object such as tumblers, mugs and glasses and threw them at the door in order to attract attention. The nurse found her and she was the last to be taken to the shelter where she spent the night. She was in considerable pain and the nurse kept an eye on her as the proud lady who had refused to travel in a German Red Cross ambulance placed a blanket over her head to hide her suffering. The pains continued and the nurse went for help.

Dina gave birth to twin boys, Peter Simon and Simon Peter. Both died within the hour on the night of the liberation.

With the capture of Tilburg by the Allies, the front line was now between Tilburg and Kaatsheuvel. The nurse brought Dina a radio with head phones and she heard that Kaatsheuvel had also been partly liberated, but that there was still fighting on the road leading to her home.

On that dark night before the final liberation of Kaatsheuvel, the house, Horst 5, was enveloped by a curtain of heavy fire, the orchard was severely damaged, the poultry loft blown away, and Simon's faithful dog tore the fences of his kennel into pieces and limped unhurt into their hiding place. The house had been badly damaged, with all the windows broken, but the surrounding trees had protected it from a direct hit. A wilderness of shot-off branches and dead and dying poultry cluttered the entrance to the shelter. On the same night Simon's old friend Piet went to see him on his bicycle, but a few yards in front of his house he met a German who ordered him to stop. He was an older man and wanted to exchange his bike for Piet's, which was of a much better quality. After some furious quarrelling Piet gave him his bike. The German was armed and Piet was not. He was convinced that he was a German soldier who had had enough of the war and wanted to get away as soon as possible on a good bicycle. Piet arrived at Simon's home on a shaky old cycle and spent that night of terror and confusion with him in his shelter.

It was a terrible night, the shellfire was intense and the screaming and the crying of the wounded could be heard even within their well-constructed shelter.

There were also, in the midst of all this carnage, acts of great humanity. At the height of the bombardment, the complex and highly civilized Simon received a request from two German soldiers of the Hermann Goering Division to be allowed to enter the cramped shelter and be protected against the raging fire. Simon agreed. Not a word was spoken and, after half an hour, they left.

In the early hours of the morning, when all was quiet again,

Piet went outside the shelter to estimate the damage. The large tree in front of the shelter had been blown to pieces, and this had probably saved their lives. He looked around a little further and saw a German soldier lying in a crater. He walked towards him thinking that he was possibly wounded and needed help. The soldier was also a member of the Hermann Goering Division and had been hit in the chest. He was dead. Piet took his identity disc from his neck in order to give it to the Red Cross. Two splendid humanitarian acts in one inhuman night of onslaught.

When the whole area was liberated, Simon cycled to Tilburg to see Dina and a few days later she was given permission to return to Kaatsheuvel. By this time most of the Germans had withdrawn as far as the River Maas which enabled Simon, Joe and a Resistance fighter to go to the German ammunition depot which was behind the garden only 700 metres away. Here they found twelve machine guns, but vital parts were missing and, as Joe was trying to assemble the guns in the kitchen, the Germans suddenly returned and a German soldier walked into the room. It appeared that the field kitchen had been hit during the retreat and all he wanted was to be given eggs and poultry. He ignored the machine guns.

The owner of the house next to the depot was told by a German officer to leave immediately as they intended to blow it up and was allowed to go to live for a while in the little house in Simon's garden. He waited until the last German had left, went back to the depot and cut all the fuses on the high explosives, thus saving all the houses in the immediate area from certain destruction.

Joe Heims reported to the Commanding Officer of the British forces and was arrested until British Intelligence was able to investigate his story. Many months later Simon and Dina received a letter from Berlin to say that he had been released and that he had married a young German girl.

The Germans left and the British arrived, placing two 25-pounder guns in the garden to attack the retreating Germans. One result was that the tiles fell off the roof of the house, but these were immediately replaced by Simon as it was beginning to snow.

The next 'guests' were Canadian soldiers who established a temporary hospital in the living room and lived in the little house in the garden. The doctor lived in the children's room and played chess with Simon in the evenings.

Simon had always been fully aware of the risks to himself and to his family if he had been discovered harbouring allied airmen. He had discussed the situation calmly with Dina and had argued that he was ideally situated to carry out this work as his house was next to an extensive forest, with no immediate neighbours, and, as the family had only recently moved from Tilburg, very few people knew him. As all cars were confiscated there would be no unwelcome visitors. These were logical arguments, used by a highly intelligent man to justify what was in reality an emotional involvement. He had identified himself with the plight of the fallen airmen and, in his own words, in a letter to me many years later, he wrote:

'But the last and most urgent turn of the scales was, "Could I say 'No' to the young people fighting for our freedom in the dark sky, when they were in trouble? I talked it over with my wife. We had four little children and it was not an easy decision, but in my home I felt a free man, and at the end it was clear that I would lose all my self-respect if I would close my door to them. My wife said 'yes', and that was the end".'

To return to my journey south. I walked on a peaceful Sunday morning into the village of Kaatsheuvel for the first time, to have my photograph taken for a hurriedly prepared new Belgian passport. I strolled along the main street without attracting any attention and entered the shop of the local photographer. Shortly afterwards I was the proud possessor of a new passport, together with a forged Belgian 'Worker's Permit'. I soon had to forget that I was Arthur Doeke, an Assistant Accountant from The Hague, and assumed my new identity as Emile Petlain, an office worker from Liège.

Simon kept a number of rabbits which supplemented the

almost negligible meat ration, but the night before leaving his impressive villa he said, 'I have for you the cock killed.'

We had a farewell feast before I left the border on the short journey to Belgium, confidently expecting to be home within a few weeks at the most. Little did I know what was in store for me.

Piet Felix arrived at five o'clock in the the morning to guide me and another evader to the Belgian border. There were no loud emotional farewells this time. The children were fast asleep, and we moved quickly and quietly on the most dangerous part of the journey. This was to be my final flight to freedom and a meticulously prepared plan was put into operation.

It was Piet's custom to have one man walking next to him, with the other following at a distance of about fifty metres, so that at least one could try to get away should anything go wrong. We set off in this formation to collect bicycles which had been left at a pre-arranged place at a crossroads approximately three hundred metres away. After only about fifty metres a group of German soldiers suddenly appeared marching from the direction of Waalwijk. Piet did not panic and assumed that before we reached our immediate destination they would have marched past us. At a command from their officer the troops came to a halt and we walked straight at them. I was about fifty metres behind and gained a little time by making what was called a 'sanitary halt'. Luckily no one panicked and nobody ran off. As we approached the Germans, conscious of the imminent danger we were in, the officer approached us and asked in a very courteous manner the way to Tilburg. Piet gave him, for once, the right directions, was thanked for his cooperation and a space was made to let us through.

At the other side of the crossroads a Resistance colleague, Hans Hoekstra, was waiting for us with the bicycles and, when the Germans were out of sight, we continued on our journey to Zundert. Piet had completed his task, but admitted to me later that he had been in a cold sweat and that this had been his most difficult assignment.

At Zundert I handed over the Dutch money and certain souvenirs which I had been given to a member of the Resistance, and was introduced to our new guide who was to take us to the border. He was to cycle a long way in front of us and we followed him for about fifty kilometres, keeping off the main roads as much as possible and travelling mostly through the woods and on cart tracks. This bid for freedom was quite exhilarating. We nearly lost our guide once. Many of the bridges over the canals opened up to allow the big barges to pass and we were approaching one bridge when this happened, delaying us for a quarter of an hour, though it seemed like an eternity.

A number of cyclists had gathered, waiting for the bridge to be lowered and we had to go back a few hundred yards lest these friendly cyclists should start talking to us. We eventually caught up with our guide who was getting very agitated as we had to be at the frontier at a precise time as it was regularly patrolled by German guards.

Another hour and we were very near the frontier. We left our bicycles in the woods and followed our guide on foot. It was agreed that if anything went wrong on the frontier he would take off his cap and we were to disappear into the woods and hide there until the same time the next day. We arrived at the border just after the patrol had moved on to another sector. The whole operation had been meticulously planned and everything went off without a hitch. At the frontier we were met by a Belgian policeman and a member of the 'Witte Brigade' – the Belgian Resistance. I had been told that this was a ruthlessly efficient organization and I was delighted to have made contact, and to be in Belgium. I was supremely confident that I would soon be home. The policeman claimed to know all there was to know about modern warfare. 'A fine Army the British,' he said, 'the Germans have nothing to compare with the new Tiger tank they have.' Why should I enlighten him by informing him that the Tiger was a German tank?

I now had to remember that I was Emile Petlain, a Belgian office worker and not Arthur Doeke the assistant accountant from The Hague. Our guide from the Witte Brigade took us to a village just inside the border and told us to stay there for an hour. We would be met by a Belgian girl who worked for the Resistance and who would help us to get to Antwerp. We hid in a hedge and, as arranged, the girl, known as Anna, came to meet us. She was attractive, neatly dressed and wore a pair of wooden shoes. She did not speak English but there was no difficulty in communication. We walked for twenty minutes to the tram terminus, but when I suggested in Dutch that we should follow her at a distance, she just laughed and said that she was not known in the area and in any case the Belgians did not ask questions.

At the terminus we had a drink and a little to eat at a small cafe. The so-called tram, belching clouds of smoke, came to an abrupt halt and we entered for the short run to Antwerp, having changed trams in a large village where there was a fair in full swing. There was a frightening degree of normality about my first glimpse of Occupied Belgium. This could have been the annual fair in Crymych or Cardigan in my native West Wales.

I sat next to a civilian and when the ticket collector came he showed him a pass bearing the insignia of the Gestapo. We got off the tram in Antwerp and I walked arm in arm with Anna to 79 Isabellalei.

CHAPTER SIX

BELGIUM

I was welcomed by my new hosts, Mr and Mrs Fernand Staquet, their son Louis and their daughter Lucy. The family lived comfortably and were generous to a fault. I was given a jar of tobacco, as many cigars as I wanted and, most important of all, a new toothbrush to replace the few bristles remaining on the one given to me during my early days in Oosterwolde.

Their son and daughter were in their early twenties and in the evening we played cards, listened to the BBC news and met some of their friends. One of them was a fluent English-speaker who had been educated at Eton. The next evening I was introduced for the first time to a man who was described as an important and active member of the Resistance, an elderly gentleman with side-burns smoking Players cigarettes. He was a very cultured man named 'Robert'.

The Staquet family and their friends were intensely pro-British and Churchill was their idol. We all listened to the BBC midnight news, and when the National Anthem was played they all stood to attention. Fernand Staquet had fought in the Belgian Army in the First World War and had been decorated for gallantry. He became active in the Resistance as early as October, 1939, although Belgium was officially a neutral country until the German occupation on 10 May, 1940. He belonged in those early days to an organization of the Resistance which clandestinely repatriated French soldiers who had inadvertently crossed the border into Belgium and would have been taken prisoner if captured. At the beginning of 1942 he was asked whether he was prepared to shelter shot-down allied airmen and, after discussing this request with Mme Staquet, and their son and daughter, he readily agreed.

M and Mme Staquet were at all times ready to welcome their 'guests', who always arrived unexpectedly. Most of them were members of the British, American and Canadian Air Forces who had been shot down over enemy territory, but half a dozen Belgian and French civilians were also hidden by them for a few days at different times. The gracious and sympathetic Staquet family made these evaders feel very much at home.

Mr and Mrs Staquet worked very closely with another Resistance friend, Mme Fernand Rahier, who on several occasions sheltered allied airmen. This tremendously courageous lady was a librarian in charge of one of Antwerp's Libraries which she used as a cover for her Resistance activities, and as there was a constant movement of people in and out of her library she felt fairly secure. Her husband was arrested in 1942 and taken to Germany as a political prisoner. When the former prisoners came home in 1945 Mme Rahier did not leave her library for three weeks so that she would be there to greet her husband. He did not return. He had died three years previously in a German concentration camp.

Fernand Staquet was in constant touch with another Resistance fighter, Mr Henri Koninckt, who had fixed a transmitter in the chandelier of his drawing room and was able to communicate with other members of the Witte Brigade over a wide area.

After the war I met for the first time six active members of the Belgian Resistance, who all testified to the significant contribution made by Fernand during these dangerous days.

To place the Belgian Resistance into some kind of perspective, there were certain sections of the community which welcomed the German invasion, in particular the Flemish National Party, the VNV and the Rexist, a small fascist party in French-speaking Belgium. The Waffen SS secured 3,500 recruits in Flemish Belgium, some of whom fought and died on the Russian front. Nevertheless, there was much more activity on the side of the Resistance with 17,000 people killed in action, or executed, or who died in the concentration camps as a result of their activities – over twice as many as had fought in German uniform.

It was the beginning of August and the war news was excellent; the Allied armies had broken through from the Caen sector and the American mechanized columns were already on the outskirts of Paris. I was convinced that it could only be a few weeks before freedom and home became a reality.

After a week in Isabellalei, Anna came to see me and said I was to meet the Head of the Resistance in Antwerp who would help me to meet the Allied armies in France. It was a glorious Sunday morning on 10 August, 1944, and, convinced that I was only a day's journey away from freedom, I joyfully bade my new friends au revoir. I was so excited, I forgot my pipe.

My instructions were these: I was to follow Anna until we came to a certain avenue where I would be handed over to the Head of the Witte Brigade. We met, Anna left us, and I followed the man to his office in a busy part of the city. He offered me a cigarette and chatted in English with a North-American accent. He told me that the Resistance was highly organized in Belgium and there would be no delay in getting me near to the Allied lines, as it would be much too dangerous to attempt to cross them at this stage. He said that he would provide me with a French passport and take me by car to a little French village near the front line, where I would wait for the Allied advance. This seemed to be an admirable plan.

He noticed that I was looking at a small German poster on the office wall depicting a German soldier in a steel helmet with his finger on his lips and the letters PST underneath. It was the German equivalent of the British security poster – 'Beware the Enemy is Listening'. He smiled and said, 'Yes, I know it may seem rather strange to you to see a German poster in the head office of the Resistance but this is just a blind. As a matter of fact the German headquarters are next door and this is the very last place that they would suspect. One of our men wears from time to time a German uniform and he will take you to France. Don't worry, we have been at this game for a long time.' This sounded very plausible and I readily accepted the explanation. I was then interrogated at length in another room where I had to prove that I was a genuine member of the RAF and not a German spy.

The interrogator assumed that I had come from Friesland and down the line and I have no difficulty in recalling his opening remarks as I had many months to dwell on them. He said, 'You come from Friesland and one of the Resistance problems in Europe is that one link works in complete ignorance of what is going on in the next. We are trying to centralize the various groups in Holland and Belgium with the Headquarters in Antwerp, and in this respect you may be able to assist us. The Witte Brigade and the Resistance movement in Holland are financially quite sound and after the war we hope to compensate all those good people who helped you, provided that they are genuine patriots. I am anxious to compile a list so that we can do this as soon as the war ends, but, if they are not sincere and cannot be trusted, I would rather not know about them. So if you would like us to help these people perhaps you would let me have their names now.' For some unknown reason I said that they had all given false names, but that I would be delighted to let him know after the war, as I was sure that they would get in touch with me.

After this interrogation I was told that there was a car waiting for me outside and, if we were stopped, to let the driver do all the talking. We drove, not towards France, but in broad daylight and in considerable style, to Antwerp Jail.

The 'Head Man of the Resistance' said, 'I am a Gestapo Officer: you wear civilian clothes to escape and I wear civilian clothes to capture you.' He clicked his heels and left.

And so ended nearly six months of successful evasion in German Occupied Europe. Some new and unpleasant experiences were about to begin.

Chapter Seven

BEHIND BARS

I had been betrayed. I found this very difficult to accept after such a long period in Occupied Europe, and with such faith in the Resistance movements. But I was in a German Orderly Room in a Belgian prison and surrounded by German guards. The initial feeling of unreality and disbelief was so great that my immediate reaction to the sight of these German guards was, 'How courageous of the Witte Brigade to be dressed in German uniform'. And then the diarrheal truth, and this feeling of disbelief was soon replaced by an intense feeling of anger, helplessness and real fear, not only for myself but also for the safety of my friends in the Netherlands and in Belgium. I will not attempt to recreate the atmosphere in this prison when the consequences of my betrayal became apparent. I had been captured in civilian clothes, with two forged passports, a Belgian Worker's Card, and had been in Occupied Europe for nearly six months. At this stage I could be treated as a spy or a saboteur. For safety, as there were frequent inspections by the Germans, especially on public transport, I had left my RAF Identity discs with Pieter Dijkstra in Garijp, and I could not prove that I was not Arthur Doeke or Emile Petlain. I was James Arthur Davies, a British subject and a legitimate member of the Royal Air Force. I had been told repeatedly in Holland that I would be leaving at my own risk, and to be caught under these circumstances could mean death. Added to this very real fear of being shot was the fear that the Germans would find out the names of the people who had helped me. There was one additional moment of near panic – the name and address of

Marianna's brother which had been sewn inside my trousers. When I was eventually allowed to go to the toilet I immediately destroyed it. I returned to the Orderly Room in a better frame of mind.

Anna was a traitor and a double agent, but my Belgian friends would not even discuss her with me on my visits to Belgium after the war. I was one of the many who gave evidence against her in the Belgian courts and she was given a long prison sentence.

I often wondered what exactly had gone wrong and how the final, vital link between Holland and Belgium had been broken. It was not until eight years ago that I received an explanation. My very dear friend, Simon de Cock, my host in Brabant, emigrated at the age of eighty to New Zealand and on 6 January, 1986, he sent me a translation of an article in the Dutch periodical *Escape,* which appeared in June, 1985. I reproduce it as it was written:

'Belgium has known a notorious traitor, namely Prosper de Zitter, a Belgian who returned from Canada shortly before the war. Already in 1940 he began collaborating with the Germans, together with his sweetheart Florentine Ginall (a divorced woman). On his conscience are one thousand Belgian Underground workers delivered to the Germans. At the same time he founded a false line of transport for Air Crew members in which over five hundred allied people (probably 250 from Holland) were trapped by the Germans.

Through this false line, they arrived at last in different houses in Antwerp and Brussels, from where they were extradited to the Germans. De Zitter worked under the names Captain Willy and Jackson. The greater part of more than one hundred aircrew members from the Dutch Underground, "Group André", crossed the border at places such as Baarle Nassau and Chaam, and were delivered by him into the hands of the Germans. Later de Zitter and his sweetheart were executed on the seventeenth of September, 1948, in Brussels.'

Another collaborator was brought to trial at the same time and was subsequently shot. He was the man I once described as 'an elderly gentleman with side-burns, smoking Players cigarettes'. He was Robert.

After a thorough search I was given a disc with a prison number on it, 698, and thrown into a filthy little cell, about eight feet by four on the third floor of Antwerp jail. It had very thick walls. I was not the first airman to enter it, and a previous occupant had written in English above the door 'Abandon Hope All Ye Who Enter Here'. It was bare but with a bucket and a wooden screen in front of it in one corner, and a dirty palliasse on the floor. I slept on the stone floor as the palliasse was alive with blood-sucking bugs. My new hosts did not provide me with water, soap or a towel. The heat was oppressive and my dirty body was swollen with bites from this insect infested cell. I can vividly recall pressing the wooden screen with my fingers and seeing trickles of blood running down the woodwork. This is not imagination. It was alive. It was grim. There was a picture of Hitler on the wall.

I wrote detailed notes on the food situation in the Netherlands when I lived there, stressing the deficiences in the diet and the harsh rationing system imposed by the Germans. I now realized for the first time that I was extremely fortunate to have been able to share their rations with these generous people and to have lived so well. My rations in Antwerp jail consisted of one cup of coffee at a quarter past six every morning without sugar or milk, one litre of turnip soup at one o'clock and in the evening two slices of bread and fat.

I shall not dwell on the few weeks of solitary confinement in this prison. The contrast was so great: one evening enjoying the comparative luxury which wealth and the Black Market could give in the then fashionable Isabellalei with the cultured Staquet family and the next alone and deprived of all the amenities which we so readily take for granted.

Through the iron bars I could see a church and could hear from time to time the disciplined chants of the choir. I was fortunate enough to have been brought up in a community which had great respect for poetry and music, so I was mentally able to escape. I was back in the Cardigan Grammar School and with the school production of Verdi's *Il Trovatore* – the Anvil scene.

One day I asked for an interview with the Commandant of this wretched prison and it was granted. I complained about the food and the sanitary conditions and quoted what I remembered about the Geneva Convention. I was dismissed in a matter of seconds. He said, 'We Germans are a clean people. These Belgian and French prisons are all the same and we did not introduce the lice. In any case you are not under international law. You are not in uniform and you are lucky that you have not been shot. You may well be. Get out.' I did.

Days of solitary confinement in a rather grim prison do not result in a feeling of benevolence towards your host and it is easy to get things out of perspective. After a week of isolation, a German guard opened the door and said 'gymnastics'. I told him what I thought of him, his Führer and his Third Reich. Then he put his hands on my shoulders and said, 'Listen, son, my name is Worfe and I was a Doctor of Philosophy and Divinity of the University of Bonn. I am not a Nazi and that is why I am only a private soldier and a medical orderly in the Army. I have nothing against the English or the Americans except that they destroy churches and monuments and things which are of historical and cultural interest to all of us.' He was a friend in a hostile environment.

Whenever he had the opportunity he would pass a German newspaper under my cell door. These newspapers contained maps of the battle front and, making full allowance for propaganda, I was again able to escape. Maps and words, even in German, created a new world outside my prison cell. I shall never forget this highly civilized and sympathetic German orderly who helped to save my sanity. He was one of the people I wanted to meet after the war, but I did not succeed in finding him. I only wanted to thank him.

One morning a very arrogant German soldier knocked on the door of my cell, came in and pushed his fingers through my hair, and shouted what I imagine was the German for haircut. I was left alone with the barber who was a Belgian. In my feeble

Dutch or Flemish I was able to understand his story. He had been caught doing acts of sabotage against the Germans and had been imprisoned. After a few months in prison, the Germans discovered that he had been a hairdresser and as a result he was to become the barber for the prisoners in Antwerp. When the German guard was out of sight, I was able to discuss my problems with him. He claimed to have been a member of the Belgian Resistance, the Witte Brigade, and as a prisoner his wife was allowed to visit him for half an hour every fortnight. He said that the next visit would be within two days. I told him that I had been betrayed by a Belgian girl and that the link had been broken. I begged of him that he should, through his wife, warn the Witte Brigade of what was happening and to cease activities for the time being. He promised faithfully that he would do this. I don't think he made it.

On my second week in prison a Belgian in German uniform brought me my daily litre of soup. I asked him why, as a Belgian, he was in German uniform and these were the reasons he gave me. 'First,' he said, 'I have a hatred of Communism. I served at the beginning of the war as a Lieutenant in the Belgian Army. When the Belgian Army was overrun and capitulated I never thought for a moment that England would fight with Russia as an ally. I fully realized the Soviet menace to Western Europe and I volunteered to fight in the German Army on the Eastern front against the Soviets, but not against the Western Allies. My request was granted and I fought in the Russian campaign. It was terrible. This was my main reason for joining the German Army, but I have to be honest and say that there was another reason. I was so disgusted with the behaviour of the British troops during their retreat from Belgium that, though I would never fight against them, I had no love for them.'

A few days later my photograph and fingerprints were taken, a record card was made out and I was marched to the prison yard. No information was given. Here I met other airmen who were in different cells and who had been shot down a few days previously. My new neighbours were Lieutenant James. R.

Brown from Mason City, Iowa, William Ballard from Kent, Leslie Woodward and Connell, two Australian Navigators, and Paddy Bailey, a Mosquito pilot who had been shot down a few days previously.

My next-door neighbours were two Russians and I saw them twice a week when we had our ten minutes of what our guards called 'gymnastics'. This involved being marched round the prison yard three times and then back to our cells. The Russians were very weak and could only manage two circuits before falling over. It was a reminder of what a long period of solitary confinement, constant interrogation and lack of food could do. I was beginning to feel weak after the first few days.

There were large numbers of German Naval deserters in one section of the prison, and I could hear and see them being drilled in the prison yard through the iron bars in my cell. The group did include one high-ranking Wehrmacht officer, and their treatment was extremely harsh. They were shouted at day and night.

There was at least one other allied airman in the same block and we communicated by tapping messages in morse code on the water pipes which linked all the cells on this floor.

One morning a German guard opened my cell door, shouted, 'Raus', and I was marched for the last time on to the prison yard. I had no idea what to expect. There were half a dozen of us of mixed nationalities, and we faced a manned machine gun. I was very much afraid and thought at one stage that this was the end. Suddenly we were pushed into a closed van and under heavy guard travelled for about three-quarters of an hour. We arrived in another Belgian prison, St Giles, in Brussels. The conditions in this prison were much better than in Antwerp. It was still solitary confinement for most of the time, but we were allowed out of our cells twice a day to join our fellow prisoners at mealtimes. What a difference it made to see others in the same predicament. Our cells were temporary ones made of wood and even in our isolation it was possible to speak to the occupant of the next cell. Prison rules were typed in English inside the door and I could call a guard by pushing a little wooden shutter in order to go to the toilet. This was a greatly appreciated luxury after the bucket arrangement in Antwerp.

I was taken before a German officer on the second day and interrogated at length. He was polite and friendly at first, but his attitude hardened when he was given the same answer to his questions: 'You as a German Officer should know that by international law I am only allowed to give you my number, rank and name'. Back to the solitary cell. He did not obtain any information and after four days I was given my final grilling. The interrogation went something like this:

'What was the number of your aircraft?'

'When were you shot down?'

'What was your target?' etc, etc.

My answer to all questions was, 'You as a German officer must know that I can only give my number, rank and name.'

'Very well then,' he said. 'If you refuse to talk I will tell you. You flew in a Lancaster Bomber, DV 237. You were shot down on 19 February on your way to Leipzig. Four of your crew are dead.' He handed me a form which I had been asked to fill in for the Belgian Resistance when I first crossed the frontier into Belgium.

I was able to convince him that I did not know the names of the people who had helped me in Holland and Belgium, as they always assumed false names, and I was moved from village to village during the hours of darkness. In the interrogation on the squadron he did not discover that I was a 'Special Duty Operator' and that we were equipped with the electronic counter-intelligence transmitter 'Airborne Cigar'. This was a tremendous relief, as these were my main worries during this uncomfortable questioning.

Two days later I was summoned to appear before the Commandant who told me that I would be taken to a prisoner of war camp in Germany, and the next day I met five other allied airmen who had recently been shot down over Belgium and who had ended up in this prison.

I was now reasonably confident that I would soon be classified as a Royal Air Force Prisoner of War, and under the protection of the Geneva Convention and the International Red Cross. Being a political prisoner in Antwerp and Brussels, and at the mercy of the local German Commandant, was an experience to be forgotten, but I had been extremely lucky. There was no international law protecting young men in civilian clothes with forged passports and I could have been shot. I thanked God and cursed the collaborators.

CHAPTER EIGHT

FROM BRUSSELS TO BANKAU

With enormous relief I left St Giles, this sinister but impressive bastion of Belgian justice, but now a German prison filled to capacity with Resistance fighters, saboteurs and others who had at different times opposed the occupying forces. The simple bilingual memorials at the two Belgian prisons of which I was a temporary resident record the heroism of the Resistance fighters and political prisoners who had been held there during the First World War as well as in the Second. I was later reminded that the fearless and dedicated nurse, Edith Cavell, had also been a prisoner at St Giles. She was the co-founder and head of a large school of nursing during the First World War and in 1914 helped fugitive soldiers to escape to neutral Holland. She was arrested and held in this prison before being tried at the Palais de la Nation where she was sentenced to death and shot on 12 October, 1915. Her brave words, 'Patriotism is not enough' are inscribed on her memorial in St Martin's Place in London. Only one word was engraved on the memorial to the political prisoners who were held in St Giles: 'Resistants'.

We were now on our way to a prisoner of war camp somewhere in Germany. Leaving Brussels station at 12.30 on 26 August, 1944, and accompanied by two armed guards, we travelled through Liège, Aachen, Cologne, Bonn and Frankfurt. For the first time I understood what it must have been like to be 'on the other side', as the result of the incredible bomb damage inflicted by the Allied Air Forces. There had been a direct hit on the bridge at Liege and burnt-out trains and locomotives riddled with cannon holes could be seen in the

Belgian rail yards. The once proud cities of Aachen and Cologne had been reduced to smouldering ruins.

We eventually arrived in Cologne where we had to wait for over an hour for our next connection, an unpleasant interval in what was otherwise a comfortable journey in an ordinary compartment which had been attached to the train.

We arrived shortly after a major air-raid on the city and, although I was still in civilian clothes, my fellow prisoners were in Air Force uniform and within minutes a group of German workers advanced on us with uncontrollable fury and truculent aggression, screaming '*Tereur fliegers*'. It was a frightening moment, and we were saved from being lynched by the highly disciplined German soldiers who kept them at bay at rifle point. We were protected by them until we were escorted into the next train which was bound for Frankfurt.

I can quite understand the attitude of these German workers and until recently I had assumed that what I witnessed on this station platform in Cologne was the spontaneous reaction of those who had suffered in the raid a few hours earlier. Jochem Von Lang, however, in his book *The Secretary. Martin Bormann; The Man Who Manipulated Hitler*, gives documentary evidence to show that there was a deliberate attempt by Bormann and Goebbels to drum up hatred and that in certain cases allied airmen who had been shot down could be killed when captured and 'that the police should not be permitted to protect their prisoners when an understandably outraged public resorted to lynching'. Late in May, 1944, Bormann issued a memorandum marked 'Secret, Not For Publication', entitled 'Justice Exercised by the People against Anglo-American Murderers'. It was an instigation to murder, but the order was largely ignored. A year later Hitler reacted furiously after the British and American squadrons bombed Dresden on 13 February, 1945, and ordered that all captured airmen should be handed over to the SD and executed by SS firing squads. The Wehrmacht decided to ignore the order.

Our own two Luftwaffe guards were middle-aged and friendly. We had our boots and trouser belts taken away and had to promise that we would not attempt to jump out of the train. We willingly agreed. It was much safer inside. One of our guards asked me whether I knew of a town in England called Reading and whether I had heard of Huntley and Palmers. When I assured him that both were well-known to me, he said, 'My uncle, he owns Huntley and Palmers'. He was a simple ground-staff Luftwaffe guard who claimed that he had shot down sixty Spitfires.

We arrived at Frankfurt-on-Main at eight o'clock in the morning and were then taken to Oberursel, a suburb about four miles north-west of the town and to Dulag Luft, short for Durchgangslager, literally throughgoing camp, or transit camp for airmen. From July, 1940, Dulag Luft became the Interrogation Centre to which all British and, later, many American Air Force prisoners were sent immediately after being shot down. Although I had already been interrogated twice and had evaded capture for six months, my reception was exactly the same as if I had baled out the previous day. After another thorough search, there were three days of isolation in a solitary cell approximately nine feet by five, with a bunk, palliasse, two blankets and a steam heater for company. This was not too difficult as I had already had a rehearsal in Antwerp and Brussel's prisons and I knew that I would soon be with other airmen and formally classified as a prisoner of war. At 6.30 the door opened and a guard provided me with a splendid breakfast – two slices of bread with black treacle and ersatz coffee, with soup for lunch, and at 7.30 another two slices of bread and margarine and a beverage which was described as tea. In sharp contrast to the conditions in Antwerp and Brussels the cell was clean and it was possible to have an undisturbed sleep on a bug-free palliasse. I was given a form to fill in with a little Red Cross on the left hand side requesting information for the Red Cross for the benefit of our families, with a hint that the sooner I provided the necessary information the sooner I would be released. This attempt at using the Red Cross as an excuse to obtain information which could have been useful to the Germans was quite unacceptable and I refused to give any information other than number, rank and name. When the interrogations were completed I was taken from the cell to the main compound at Oberursel where I joined the other prisoners of RAF Bomber and Fighter Command. I was now with my own people. There was almost a feeling of liberation, but I was still deep inside the Third Reich and the future was uncertain.

We lived in wooden barracks surrounded by barbed wire defences in the main compound, but our living quarters were far superior to anything which we experienced later. During this short stay we received the standard German rations of a fifth of a loaf a day, potatoes, a small portion of meat, turnip soup and the inevitable sauerkraut, supplemented by an adequate supply of Red Cross food parcels. The Germans treated us well, possibly in order to create an atmosphere in which the prisoners would talk freely about their experiences, and hopefully their squadrons. We had already been prepared for this subtle attempt at initial doctrination by an Intelligence Office in faraway Lincolnshire. The plentiful supply of Red Cross parcels was aimed at proving to the International Red Cross authorities that we were guests of a civilized nation which rigidly adhered to the requirements of the Geneva Convention.

After a few nights in the main compound, about twenty of us marched to the station where we boarded a train for the very short journey to the transit camp at Wetzlar. After the tensions, difficulties and uncertainties of the past few weeks, this was almost a holiday camp. The endless interrogations and long periods in solitary confinement were over. I was taken to the Red Cross stores in the main compound where I was given a suitcase, which included luxuries such as soap, a razor, certain articles of clothing and a letter card to write home. There was even a distribution of cigarettes, a pair of boots, and a printed warning that if we attempted to escape on our long journey to our prison camp in Poland we would be shot:
'The Geneva convention says we must give a warning before shooting an escapee, so I now give you that warning: if you try to escape you will be shot.'

My very expensive black-market blue sports suit which had

been given to me by the Resistance in Friesland was replaced by a mongrel uniform consisting of RAF trousers and an American tunic. Arthur Doeke/Emile Petlain was now officially RAF Prisoner 698. After a week thirty of us marched to the station carrying our precious Red Cross case and a food parcel for the long train journey to a permanent prisoner of war camp, Stalag Luft 7, in Bankau near Kreuzburg, fifty miles east of Breslau in Poland, then Upper Silesia. We arrived at Luft 7 two days later.

CHAPTER NINE

STALAG LUFT 7

We marched into the outer compound and again experienced the usual German formalities – searches, documentation, finger-printing, and eventually after numerous recounts we were allowed into the main compound where we met our fellow prisoners of RAF Bomber and Fighter Command, and later, Army Glider pilots, sad survivors of the tragic Arnhem disaster. The first airmen arrived in June, 1944, and by January, 1945, there were over a thousand prisoners.

Luft 7 was the last RAF prisoner of war camp to be built and the work had not been completed when we arrived. I suppose it was similar in construction to the other camps, but the Germans had now perfected their anti-escape procedures. Security was extremely tight, and there is no record of a successful escape from this heavily defended camp. In the centre of the compound were the rows of wooden huts in which we lived, and outside there was an open space about fifty yards wide. Between the double wire of the perimeter fence and the open space the ground was thick with loose coils of barbed wire, and immediately inside the barbed wire there was an area of about ten yards of dead ground. If we crossed this we would be shot without warning. Beyond the dead ground over a thousand frustrated prisoners gazed longingly at potato-picking Polish women in the nearby fields. There was a lot of barbed wire in between.

About one hundred yards or so beyond the perimeter fence stood the watch towers, known to us as the 'Goon boxes'. The interior of the camp was completely covered by machine guns manned by the 'Goons'. At night the boundary lights lit up the perimeter and the whole camp was illuminated by powerful searchlights from the watch towers.

'Goon' was the term used for all Germans, the original Goon being a sub-human being in a *Daily Mirror* cartoon. In addition to the guards on the outside of the wire and those in the watch towers, five or six special security men, known as 'Ferrets', were assigned to each compound with at least two on duty throughout the hours of daylight. In *A Short Kriegie Dictionary*, "Ferret" was defined as 'A burrowing variety of goon species, wears blue overalls and utters loud cries on discovering Kriegie tunnels'. At night, in addition to the guards who patrolled the compound with dogs all glistening with teeth, a "ferret" would also make frequent visits. The "ferrets' were everywhere, spoke English and tried to ingratiate themselves with the prisoners in order to obtain information on any proposed nefarious acts.

After months of endangering the lives of my friends in the Netherlands and Belgium, it was a tremendous relief to have arrived at a proper Prisoner of War Camp, and to be surrounded by fellow airmen. This was an unexpected bonus after the grim isolation and uncertainty of the political prisons of Antwerp and Brussels.

In 1971, the Editor of the Journal of the Association of Education Committees, *Education*, invited three former members of the Armed Services to contribute an article on 'Wartime Christmases Remembered'. In my letter of acceptance I wrote, 'There are thousands better qualified than I am to write on prisoner-of-war life, therefore I shall be very brief.' It is even more true today as this experience has been well documented in recent years. Having written my few thoughts on this period, I read *Escape From Germany*, the extremely eloquent book by Aidan Crawley. He reminds us that there were ten thousand British Air Force prisoners in permanent camps in Germany in the Second World War and less than thirty ever reached Britain or a neutral country after escaping.

Although fully aware of the difficulties of breaking out of a heavily defended prisoner of war camp, and travelling through Germany to a neutral or liberated country, all RAF prisoners regarded it as their duty to try to escape, and also to make life as difficult as possible for their captors. Our first objective was not achieved. Our pathetic tunnel collapsed in the sandy Silesian soil. Our guards never understood our twisted sense of humour and were very confused when they saw a notice in front of the abandoned tunnel: 'Tunnelling in progress – please keep out.'

There was one clever escape attempt, though I did not witness it. There were occasional camp concerts and it was good policy to invite our German hosts. The Escape Committee had been active for many months and some of the members had made a replica of a German officer's uniform out of odd bits of clothing. It was complete with the correct insignia and an imitation revolver made of wood. Three German officers accepted the invitation to witness the artistic talents of the decadent British. A few minutes before the end of the performance, the prisoner walked calmly through the main gate, muttering in German about the so-called 'culture' of the English prisoners. The guard saluted and the disguised airman went through the main gate, out of the compound. Ten minutes later the three genuine German officers left the concert hall. Complete chaos. The airman was soon captured and placed in the 'cooler' but it was worth the effort. The attempts to escape, even if unsuccessful, were of some military value, as hundreds of German soldiers were deployed in trying to capture escaped prisoners instead of fighting on the Eastern or Western Fronts.

Leaflets were distributed by the Germans warning the prisoners of the dangers of trying to escape. Under the bold heading 'To all Prisoners of War – The escape from prison camps is no longer a sport!' there followed a statement that a "confidential military pamphlet entitled 'The Handbook of Modern Irregular War' proved that the British had opened up a non military form of gangster war."

According to the Goebbels Diaries, which were edited by Hugh Trevor-Roper, the following entry appears on Sunday, 4 March, 1945: 'Goebbels had proposed in February, 1945, that Hitler should denounce the Geneva Convention and order that all the British and Americans in prisoner of war camps be shot.

This, he said, would both stop the Allied bombing and deter German soldiers from surrendering in the West, lest they be treated likewise. Those already captured could be written off.'

If we failed in our first objective, we certainly succeeded in the second and we made life as difficult as possible for the prison camp authorities. Just one example will suffice. We all had to parade every morning in order to be counted. An operation which could be carried out in a matter of minutes took many hours in the bitterly cold winter of 1944–45. All attempts at getting a correct count were sabotaged as prisoners would double up and move from one column to the next. The guards were not amused and many of these morning inspections ended up in utter confusion. Invariably, one or two airmen would end up in the cooler.

I remember the climax of a very frustrating morning for the guards when three prisoners were dragged before the officer in charge. One gave his number and name as Whitehall 1212, the next as Donald Duck and the third as Mickey Mouse. Adolescent humour but good for morale.

I was recently reminded by Doug Schofield, who occupied a bunk in Room 13 in the same block, of the attempt made to dig a tunnel to coincide with preparations for an ice-rink outside the window. The idea was to dispose of the earth which was being dug out from under the fireplace in order to create a hiding place in which some prisoners could be concealed until the Russians arrived. The plan was not successful and we were all evacuated.

RAF Aircrew were all commissioned or non-commissioned officers and were therefore not allowed to work outside the camp or to leave the compound. In this respect we were, as prisoners of war, at a serious disadvantage in comparison with the other ranks who worked on the land, and even in the mines in Poland, and who were able to supplement the camp rations with food scrounged during their hours outside the camp. The Geneva Convention laid down that the rations provided by the German authorities were to be of the same quality and quantity as those issued to the German depot troops, but in practice the

25. Russian soldiers at Luckenwolde camp en route for Berlin.

26. Settling old scores after the Liberation.

27. A village welcome. Boncath, Pembrokeshire, welcomes a homecoming prisoner of war.

28. Piet Felix *(standing) (see p 81)* celebrating the Liberation with the De Cock family, May, 19⁴

Reunion, 1946. Front Row: Vrouw Rinse Postma, Rinse Postma, and Vrouw Dijkstra.
Back Row: Pieter Dijkstra, Author's mother, Author and Elisabeth Dijkstra.

Tolbert honours three of the crew of K-King, 1947.

31. The author revisits St Giles Prison, Brussels.

32. The scene of the crash revisited fifty years later. *Left to right*: Andries Van Der Donk, autl
Betsy Visser de-Jong, Jaap Boersma.

German food rations were the lowest grade, only adequate for those who were too old to work.

The Welsh Society had the very good fortune to have one of its members, R. F. Lloyd, in charge of the cook-house. He tended to favour his fellow countrymen. According to my fellow prisoner, Bill Williams, the German food ration was a sixth of a loaf per man per day, a litre of turnip soup and five potatoes. Without the occasional Red Cross parcel we would have been in very serious difficulties. We should have received one Red Cross parcel a week, but this never happened. Even one parcel a month made all the difference between severe malnutrition and a tolerable diet. We were not at any time very hungry, though problems arose from the temptation to eat too much and all at once when the Red Cross parcels did arrive.

I am not particularly interested in the attention given nowadays to eating a 'balanced diet', or on the number of calories per day a man should eat in order to be reasonably fit, though I should be, as I have now reached the biblical target of seventy. Therefore, I shall quote again Aidan Crawley in his report to the Government:

'An average-size man leading the sort of life that is possible for a prisoner of war confined within a camp needs three thousand calories a day for full health. Had prisoners been able to sleep for the greater part of each twenty-four hours, they could have lived healthily on one thousand six hundred calories. The German rations averaged about one thousand six hundred calories a day and occasionally sank as low as eleven hundred calories. The deficiency had to be made good from other sources – Red Cross food parcels. The closer the Allied ring tightened around Germany the more dislocated transport became and the more irregular the parcels. In the winter of 1944 parcels failed to arrive for several months. The food value of the Red Cross parcel was approximately 1,280 calories per day. When prisoners were getting a whole parcel a week, therefore, in addition to their German ration, they were being fed adequately, but there was no single year of the war in which Red Cross parcels arrived so regularly that the full diet was available throughout.

With anything less than a whole parcel a week a prisoner suffered from a greater or lesser degree of malnutrition.'

On average, we each received one parcel a month.

The routine of camp life consisted of morning and afternoon *Appel* parades, walking round the compound, always anticlockwise and usually in pairs, known as 'circuit bashing', the collection of the daily rations and the never-to-be-forgotten moments of great drama when we received the Red Cross food parcels. These came from the United Kingdom, Canada and the United States of America and, depending on the origin, contained supplies of tinned foods, butter, chocolate and cigarettes. In all the barrack rooms the 'compound' system was well established, a term used for a collection of people who had agreed to mess and eat together. This could range from two persons or, as in many cases, the whole room. Whatever the system, one person only had to be nominated to collect the German rations from the kitchen, usually daily at twelve noon.

It was in Barrack Block 8 that I first met Phil Potts, a Navigator, who became my constant companion on our daily circuit bashing, when we discussed profound political and philosophical questions which helped to liberate us from this artificial barbed-wired community. Phil was shot down in a Lancaster on 18 August, 1944, on a raid to wipe out a German rocket-launching site on the Pas de Calais. In spite of being hit by flak, the bombing run was completed, the bombs dropped and the photograph taken. Within seconds, the whole of the wing inboard engine was ablaze and it was obvious that they could not continue to fly. The Skipper gave the order to bale out, but, as he could still control the aircraft, all crew members acknowledged the order and prepared to abandon the aircraft. The order of exit was first the Bomb Aimer, who removed the hatch as he was already in the nose, second the Flight Engineer who was standing next to the pilot, and third the Navigator. As the third man out, Phil waited until the Mid-Upper Gunner appeared over the main spar as the Rear Gunner had already been killed. He then jumped through the hatch. So far the 'evacuation' had been carried out strictly according to the approved procedures and all members of the crew had responded to the Skipper's command to bale out. Phil jumped out at about 3,000 feet and saw one other parachute at a much lower level. He had to 'slide-slip' his parachute to avoid landing on or near the aircraft, but to his horror, before he reached the ground, the aircraft disintegrated in a mass of flames with ammunition exploding in all directions. There were two men still inside, and Phil never understood why they decided to stay in the aircraft, contrary to instructions.

There was plenty of time to think and to talk, and on the circuit we prepared blue-prints for the brave new post-war world which would emerge after the destruction of an all-embracing apparatus of terror and repression in Europe.

A few years later Maurice Ginsberg, the Martin White Professor of Sociology at the London School of Economics, attempted to enlighten his students on some of the topics we discussed as we walked around the compound in Silesia. I was well prepared for these stimulating lectures on 'Reason and Unreason in Society', especially the ones on 'National Character', 'Anti-Semitism', 'Moral Progress' and 'The Causes of War'. I had scribbled under the notes on 'The Causes of War' a quotation from Grotius, who wrote in the 17th century: 'Throughout the Christian World I observed a lack of restraint in relation to war, such as even barbarous races should be ashamed of. I observe that men rush to arms for slight causes, or no cause at all, and that when arms have once been taken up there is no longer any respect for law divine or human.'

Within this secure and well constructed wooden hut, there were six double bunks, a small table, a smaller window, and an impressive wood-burning stove, which was largely decorative, as our hosts did not think that it was necessary to provide us with wood. Block 8 was occupied by two Polish fighter pilots who slept in the bunk above mine, and who snored, five Englishmen, three Welshmen, and one Australian.

I can now only recall four, in addition to Phil – the Australian, Leslie Woodward, who had previously occupied the next cell in St Giles prison in Brussels, a Welshman, Arthur

Davies from Bridgend, a dark gypsy looking character from Liverpool, and a very sophisticated Englishman, Bridgeman, known to us as 'The Count', who told us that he would entertain us to a six-course dinner when the war was over, as his uncle owned an internationally acclaimed London hotel. We accepted the invitation. We are still waiting.

Later, the twelve of us were joined by three Army Glider pilots, fortunate survivors of the Battle of Arnhem, code-named 'Market Garden', the airborne operation in which Allied paratroops were to seize key river crossings in advance of British Second Army tanks. The British paratroops were over-whelmed by a ferocious German counter-attack. They held out for ten days instead of the two which had been planned. 2,200 survivors were evacuated, leaving 7,000 killed, 33,400 wounded, and 21,000 captured or missing. 'Market Garden', a plan to bring the war in Europe to an early end – was a gamble that failed. One of the three captured glider pilots in our hut had served in the regular army in pre-war India, and in this confined space we could not escape his graphic and highly improbable account of his life in the Army on the North West Frontier. We were also joined by an RAF Warrant Officer navigator, whose experiences were largely confined to the Highlands of Scotland.

There were many activities other than card games, and many prisoners of war in the various camps, especially those who had spent nearly five years behind the wire, used this long period for creative and educational pursuits.

Lance-Sergeant Fred Mulley of the Worcestershire Regiment was a prisoner of war in Germany from 1940 until 1945, and during this period he studied and obtained a London University BSc (Economics) Degree as an external student by correspon-dence courses through the agency of the British Red Cross. In 1945 he was accepted as an adult scholar in Oxford and graduated with First Class Honours in Philosophy, Politics and Economics. He later became an MP and held numerous Minis-terial posts, and when I became a member of an educational deputation to the House of Commons in 1975 we were received by the Secretary of State for Education and Science, The Right Honourable William Frederick Mulley, now Lord Mulley.

Peter Thomas was an RAF prisoner of war from 1941 until the end of the war in Europe. During his captivity he played an active part in the theatrical and artistic life of the camp. His contribution was recorded by another prisoner, Frank Taylor, in his book *Barbed Wire and Footlights*, and together they made a significant contribution to the maintenance of morale under difficult circumstances. Frank recalls this activity: 'Some of the leading lights from the adjoining compound came over to see my production and among the notables were Peter Thomas and Roy Dotrice, now one of England's leading actors. Before they left they told me that they were lucky enough to have in their possession a microphone and a speaker as part of their theatre equipment, so I suggested we did a deal – my *Sixteen Famous American Plays* for their sound equipment. After agreeing on a four weeks' time limit and a date for mutual exchange they returned to their own compound. The result of this highly satisfactory arrangement was their presentation of *Front Page* and my radio production of John Galsworthy's *Escape*.'

Twenty years later a former prisoner from Luft 7 came to see me with a plea for help, as he had never recovered from his experiences on the forced march from Poland, and had not succeeded in obtaining a war pension. I wrote to a fellow prisoner who was in the next camp with the result that my friend was employed in a post which gave him years of satisfying service. The fellow prisoner was now The Right Honourable Peter John Mitchell Thomas PC, QC, who became Secretary of State for Wales between 1970 and 1974. He is now Lord Thomas of Gwydyr.

I have referred to two former 'kriegies' who became Cabinet Ministers, and I like to believe that their enforced captivity may even have helped them in their illustrious careers. There was another prisoner, probably unknown, but who is more than worthy of a mention. I would very much like to have met him. Sergeant R. P. L. Mogg was shot down over Germany and taken prisoner early in the war. In captivity he was able to express his feelings in poetry, and a fellow prisoner, Sergeant J. W. Lambert, illustrated two memorable poems which were reproduced in facsimile as they were sent from the prisoner of war camp via the Red Cross in 1943. I came across this beautifully illustrated book of poems *For This Alone and Other Poems* just before being demobilized from Sunning Hill Park in Berkshire in 1946. Sergeant Mogg discovered that he had a considerable amount of time to indulge in literary diversions, and his poem 'Heldentod' was set to music by another prisoner of war, Sergeant H. W. Bradley.

In the Introduction to the book, Edward Alderton wrote in October, 1943: 'It is possible that he might be accused of being morbid but the dividing line between operational flying and Death is of a very nebulous character'. The Poet reminded us of our youth:

> Was it for this alone
> we left the darkness of the womb,
> To go,
> but children still
> into the lofty places of the Gods.
>
> To play
> among the towered cumulus,
> and flirt
> along the pillared ramparts of the storm
> To watch great clouds
> flower in ever-changing shapes.
>
> And see
> black crossed, sharp silhouettes
> across our sights
> spin
> flaming down.
>
> And then
> to know the same fleet death.

The sweet sharp agony.
The searing change
from eager life
back to the shadowed mystery of Oblivion.

The literary diversions of the majority of prisoners were the heavily censored letters to our homes. We were allowed to write, in pencil, two letters and four postcards a month, and very often there were many months before they reached their destination. I still have the nine letters and seven postcards which I wrote to my parents as they were carefully preserved by my mother. My first card was posted on 26 August, 1944, and was received by them on 12 January, 1945, in which I stated that I was perfectly healthy and unwounded and that our treatment was 'honestly very good'. The next two lines on this official postcard had been erased by the censor.

Aidan Crawley in his report to the Air Ministry offered an explanation for this long delay. It appears that censorship became the responsibility of the Camp Commandant, and that all letters, books and pamphlets were scrutinized by a staff of German girls working under German officers, and a selection of each was sent to the head Censorship Office in Berlin. All the cards and the one-page letter cards had to be written in English, but I was able to give my parents some indication as to the location of the present camp by introducing an occasional word in Welsh. For example, 'We sang all the old songs in the Welsh Club, such as Aberystwyth and *"Byddin Rwsia Bron A Cyrraedd"* (The Russian army nearly here).'

I did not receive any letters from home although my parents had written every week, and this lack of communication was a constant source of worry.

My contribution to the Journal *Education* appeared on Christmas Eve, 1971, the year in which the proposed membership of the United Kingdom in the European Common Market was being hotly debated. Under the title 'Davies: Welsh Hymns in Luft 7' I wrote:

'It was Christmas in a prisoner of war camp in Eastern Europe near the Czechoslovak – Polish border. We were nearly all members of the Royal Air Force and Allied air crews together with some of the survivors of the Arnhem airborne disaster, an international community of Czechs, Poles, Latvians and representatives of the Air Forces of the British Empire. It was my privilege to have been the founder and chairman of a significant minority group in this camp – the Luft 7 Welsh Society. There were 39 members, and on the morning parade the senior officer would read a long list of announcements, such as that D Hut would be deloused at 1800 hours but nearly always ending with some reference to the Welsh Society. Our activities were almost entirely educational and cultural and our one effort at tunnelling was a dismal failure. The soil was sandy and the tunnel collapsed. We were much more successful in the teaching of Welsh as a second language to our friends from the Anglicized parts of Wales and a dozen Australians and Canadians who had married Welsh girls and were determined not to be at a linguistic disadvantage. The Welsh choir came up to all expectations and we took our practices very seriously. We were without a piano and without music and unfortunately not one of the owners of those fine voices could transcribe and arrange our favourite songs into four parts. We recruited an Englishman to help us – Arthur Horsman – a gifted professional musician who willingly performed this task for us. Our signature tune was "Cwm Rhondda" and our repertoire included "Aberystwyth", "Ton y Botel", and the Horsman Special – "Blow, blow, breathe and blow, wind of the Western Sea".

'Our great moment came at the Christmas concert with the German guards standing to attention as we sang "*Gad i'm deimlo awel o Galfaria fryn*". We repaid the compliment with an attempt at "*Heilige Nacht*". Even Fred, the German goon, appeared to be moved, though he had gone beserk a few days previously because he kept counting one too many on the morning parade.

'It had been snowing steadily all day. The Russians were breaking through on the Eastern Front and our spiritualist friends, who relied on sources from another world for their information, said that they were now only 160 kilometres away.

'There was one fatality on Christmas Day, a young air-gunner who had hoarded his rations of Red Cross food for months to have a Christmas feast and died of what was called a "blockage".

'This Christmas was memorable because a small group of patriotic Welshmen were made aware of the fact that they also belonged naturally to a European tradition. It is a pity that the so-called great debate on the Common Market has degenerated into an argument over the price of pork and the future of fish. It is also sad that our friends from the East will not have a part to play in it.'

'Our friends from the East.' Thirty-seven years later, at an international conference in Soest in Germany, I had the honour of welcoming delegates from Estonia, Latvia, Lithuania, Hungary, and Czechoslovakia to their first Conference in Western Europe. Our friends from the East had arrived, heralding a new and, let us hope, a war-free Europe.

I have the original Minute Book with the names of all the members of the Luft 7 Welsh Society, and in January, 1978, three of the members came to see us in our home in Bangor. Iorwerth Roberts, the *Daily Post* reporter, heard about this visit, and under the heading, 'Four Men and Memories' wrote as follows:

'As reunions go, it was not the biggest nor the most important of the year. There were only four men present, four men who had shared experiences 34 years ago, in prisoner of war camps, four men who had faced death in each other's company. They are all RAF veterans, and they either baled out or crash-landed over enemy territory in World War 2. And they were all in Stalag Luft 7 somewhere in Poland.

They all met together in 1944. They are all Welsh, and they belonged to Luft 7 Welsh Society back in those dark days. Jim Davies was the Society's Chairman, Emrys Williams was its Secretary, Noel Morris was the Choir Master, and Bill Williams a chorister.'

They deserve more than this. Emrys Williams (Embo) was flying one of eight Mustang P51 fighter planes acting as top cover to other Mustangs involved in the low level bombing of railway lines near Dreux in France on 24 June, 1944. It was just another mundane operation and his thoughts were more on the possible evening 'thrash' than on the immediate exercise, as he had failed to entice into action any German fighters for many weeks. Suddenly he was 'bounced' by 34 Messerschmitt Bf 109s and Focke-Wulf 190s. He was shot down, of all places, within half a mile of the German Luftwaffe Headquarters of the Squadron that had not only shot him down, but three other members of 65 Squadron. Embo was the only survivor.

Today Embo only has a faint scar on his forehead, but for many years it was a very deep gash, and he has nothing but praise for the German Luftwaffe Medical Staff, headed by an Austrian Medical Officer, who gave him first-class medical attention. He also received visits from the German fighter-squadron pilots and also from the man who had shot him down. We in Bomber Command were regarded as 'tereur fliegers', but there was still an element of comradeship amongst the fighter boys on both sides, though this may be a generalization based on the evidence of the few fighter pilots I know.

Embo was the guest of his adversaries until he was well enough to be transferred to a prisoner of war camp and, after four days in the dungeons of Chartres prison, he arrived in Dulag Luft for a further eight days of solitary confinement, before arriving at Luft 7, where he was elevated to the rank of Secretary to the Welsh Society.

He will not be remembered for the gash on his forehead but for another distinguishing characteristic on another part of his anatomy, and I must now refer to the most significant code name in the history of Stalag Luft 7 – 'Fagin'. There were other code names used by the armed forces during the Second World War and these have been well documented, such as 'Overlord', the code name for the Normandy invasion in June, 1944, 'Market Garden', the Allied attempt to seize the bridges across the Dutch rivers in September, 1944, and 'Thunderclap', the Allied attack on Dresden in February, 1945. Those of us who were Special Duty Operators also had to memorize the German codes in the electronic intelligence war, such as 'Otto, Otto' (aircraft held in searchlight), 'Reise Reise' (Return to base), and 'Pauke, Pauke Machen' (Aircraft turn to attack). The military historians were not aware of code name 'Fagin'.

The Germans allowed us to have hot showers on very rare occasions and these were restricted to two minutes per group. My good friend Embo had been cursed since school days with what the medical profession called a 'hydrocele' – a slight swelling of the left testicle, but it was not sufficiently noticeable to cause serious comment during his early years of RAF service. Whatever the cause, the air crash or the enforced diet, the testicle became alarmingly swollen and, according to the owner, 'reached a size sufficient to fill a pint pot'. The Goons in charge of the showers, convinced of the superiority of the Herrenvolk, were mesmerized by this vastly superior Welsh testicle, and the two minutes stretched to four minutes, a fact which was not missed by his so-called friends and room-mates. According to Ted Sergeant, another Fighter Pilot who occupied the same hut, there was a desperate attempt to get into Embo's group in order to enjoy that extra two minutes of luxury. Embo's unfortunate appendage, for secrecy code-named 'Fagin' was not a war-winner, but a tremendous morale-booster on those infrequent occasions when we enjoyed the luxury of a hot shower. I have not finished with 'Fagin' and more will be revealed.

I had assumed that all of us who were guests of the Führer in Stalag Luft 7 were there as the result of enemy action, but there was one notable exception, our Choir Master, Noel Morris. Noel was a Spitfire pilot engaged in Photographic Reconnaissance based at RAF Station, Northolt, in the summer of 1944, when the allied invasion forces were encountering serious setbacks and severe resistance from the Germans on the French coast. Photographic Reconnaissance operations were carried out at high altitudes in Spitfires or Mosquitos modified with extra fuel tanks in lieu of armament. Occasionally there would be a need for a low level sortie referred to by the pilots as a 'dicer'. Clipped-wing versions of the Spitfire V would be used on these 'dicers' and the aircraft were armed.

At this time, experiments with aviation 100-octane fuel were taking place, and the lead content was being increased, with the result that the hitherto very reliable Rolls Royce Merlin engine became prone to sudden failure. Given sufficient height, the pilot was supposed to deal with the problem by cutting back the power and switching off the magnetos, allowing about ten seconds for smoke and flames to subside, then switching on again and gradually opening up the throttle.

This was the theory and the scientists were frantically trying to resolve the problem. But the little 'gremlins' besetting the noble Merlin engine had other ideas. On 22 July, 1944, Noel went on a 'dicer' to Doullens to photograph the condition of the bridge. Large concentrations of enemy troops were known to be in the surrounding countryside, with a well-concealed missile-launching site near the bridge. He was within two or three minutes of the target when he felt a slight 'miss' from the engine and saw a puff of white smoke from the exhaust. A quick check around the instruments seemed to indicate that all was well, and then it happened – dead silence from the Merlin, white smoke changing to black, with flames shooting out from the exhaust. Through the smoke he could see a large field of corn which had been partly cleared, leaving a long strip of stubble. The actual landing was better than he had expected, but the deceleration was so sudden that his canopy shot forward with a terrific bang and all his efforts to open it were in vain. He was now securely trapped in a burning aeroplane. Placing both feet on the instrument panel, he grabbed hold of the canopy release handle, and with the strength of a desperate man, it came away. He dived out and sprinted towards the uncut corn. A few seconds later his Spitfire blew up.

He heard the whine of a bullet close to his ear and, on looking around, he could see a soldier in field-grey, lining up for a second shot. He raised his arms to show that he was unarmed, another five soldiers appeared and there was no escape. He was now on his interrupted journey to the infamous interrogation centre at Dulag Luft.

After interrogation by a junior officer of the Wehrmacht at a field command post, he was taken in a small truck with two guards to a large French chateau somewhere near Abbeville, commandeered as the Army Headquarters, where he experienced an allied air raid and dived into a trench with his guard. After ten minutes they heard the all-clear, and one or two of the soldiers thought it hilarious when they saw Noel helping his guard to clamber out of the trench.

His next move was to a little French prison, where he appeared to be the only customer. As might be expected, his morale was at a very low ebb and he lay awake at night wondering how long the war would last. The following morning he awoke to see that sunlight from the little window was lighting up a square patch on the wall. Looking closer, he could see that someone had written the 23rd Psalm on that sunny patch, and underneath was written 'Dunkirk 1940'. From that point, morale was restored.

Two days later he was joined by another prisoner, a pilot in the Fleet Air Arm, and they were ordered into a large canvas-covered lorry. Two soldiers armed with automatic rifles joined them, and at the front end of the lorry there were two brand new coffins, crudely built of elm. One of the Germans pointed to the coffins with his gun and then pointed at each of the two prisoners in turn. After a tense fifteen minutes they arrived at a small village, where the Germans dropped the tail-board of the lorry and unloaded the coffins near the village hall. The guards looked at the two prisoners, killing themselves with laughter. In another half hour they arrived at a railway station where they were handed over to another two German guards, their age and medal ribbons indicating that they were veterans of the First World War. Hours later they arrived at the Gare du Nord in Paris, where a young Nazi Officer walked up to Noel, stopped, cleared his throat, spat on the wings on his tunic and walked away without a word. The elderly veteran said, 'Nein, nein,' and produced a clean handkerchief to wipe away the spit.

Outside the station he was placed in a coach which was already occupied by a captured Australian bomber crew, and from there to Brussels, and the next day to the Interrogation centre at Frankfurt-on-Main and Dulag Luft. After solitary confinement for 21 days, when no information was given apart from number, rank and name, he joined the others at the transit camp, and finally reached Stalag Luft 7.

One day he spotted a notice inviting all the Welshmen to meet on a certain day, with the intention of setting up a Welsh Club. This is when we met and how he became the conductor of our Welsh Choir.

On Christmas Day, 1944, Noel conducted our little choir when we entertained our fellow prisoners, and even the German officers rose to their feet to join in a standing ovation.

Many years later I discovered that this was not his first Christmas under unusual circumstances. On Christmas Day, 1943, dressed in a borrowed dinner jacket, he was entertained to lunch at the British Embassy in Madrid by the British Ambassador to Spain, Sir Samuel Hoare. Our versatile conductor had been shot down in his Spitfire during a low-level sortie over the south of France, evaded capture, crossed the Pyrenees into neutral Spain, reported at the Embassy, and after nearly a month as a temporary member of the Embassy staff, was flown home from Gibraltar to join his previous squadron.

The two Christmases could not have been more different, and although he enjoyed the good life in neutral Spain in 1943 with rich food and sophisticated company, he still remembers with great pride the way in which, under his baton, a small group of fellow countrymen were able to make a temporary escape from an uncertain environment and a very doubtful future. He was proud of his little choir and loud in his praise of a man I shall call Ifan, who had an impressive tenor voice, was an invaluable member of his choir and a staunch supporter of our little society.

This invaluable member of Noel's choir appeared in our camp under rather mysterious circumstances. Whereas we had marched to Luft 7 in groups under armed guard, and in a variety of uniforms, Ifan came alone. A tall immaculately dressed airman, he arrived in what appeared to be a brand new RAF uniform and with a pair of expensive kid-gloves, which were certainly not standard service issue. His first language was Welsh, but he was also fluent in German and was on extremely friendly terms with the guards. He was placed in the same hut as Phil, who was envious of his gloves, but highly critical of his general attitude towards the other occupants of the hut, as he made no attempt to integrate.

We were not completely at ease in the company of the plausible extrovert with the fine voice, who on many occasions told me that he could help me to escape as he had good contacts outside the wire. There was something wrong and we communicated our vague suspicions to the Camp Leader. There were so many unanswered questions; where did the gloves come from? How did he arrive on his own? Where had he been previously? And how did an air-gunner from a small Welsh town who was shot down on his twentieth birthday acquire such a mastery of the German language?

Our activities as a Club came to an end when the camp was evacuated and I did not see Ifan again until a few months later, after the long wait for liberation, when we were eventually flown to Brussels. We were now free, but the Military Police were there to receive him, and he was immediately placed under arrest. His Court Martial was given wide publicity in the national and regional newspapers in August, 1945. He appeared in court wearing RAF battledress with an air-gunner's badge and a service ribbon, and pleaded 'Not Guilty' to eleven charges. After three sessions, the Court found him 'Not Guilty' on six charges, two of which were punishable by death, but guilty on the following four charges:

'Aiding the enemy by asking prisoners of war to give information regarding RAF formations; making German propaganda records at the Rundfunkhaus; lending money to persons engaged in the formation of the British Free Corps; accepting employment from the German Foreign Office at 350 marks a month; and from Radio Metropole at 600 marks.'

A confused catalogue of intrigue, fantasy and facts emerged from his prepared statements which were read in the Court and from his replies during forty-five minutes in the witness box. Ifan informed the Court that he had baled out of a blazing Lancaster which had bombed the V weapon station at Peenemunde on the night of 17–18 August, 1943, seven days after his twentieth birthday. He arrived at Dulag Luft, the Interrogation Centre, on 21 August, 1943. It was at this Centre that he first collaborated by asking prisoners of war on behalf of the German authorities to fill in the answers on the so-called Red Cross forms which he well knew contained questions as to RAF formations. He now operated under the name Herr Becker and was known as Becker by the German staff. From 16 October, 1943, until 8 August, 1944, he became involved in the activities of the British Free Corps and claimed that he had been offered an immediate commission in this organization which was intended to be used to fight with the German army against the Russians. He met their leaders, now under the name of John Charles Baker, and posed as a Government official and an important person in the German Foreign Office. He lent money to members of the British Free Corps and also provided them with revolvers which he obtained, according to his statement, from a Dutch doctor in a 'dive' in Spandau, a Berlin suburb, with money from the Foreign Office. During this period Ifan produced some talks for broadcasting at his furnished office in Berlin. In view of his membership of the Luft 7 Welsh Society, I can not resist quoting the following statement which he made at his Court Martial:

'It was arranged for me to go to the Radio Metropole broadcasting station at Wannsee. After I had been there for a time I told them I spoke Welsh and as there were Welsh regiments in Italy and Africa, I suggested that I should do broadcasts in Welsh. I wrote a script with the Welsh national anthem, "Land of my fathers", then I gave an address which included the Lord's Prayer, and in the middle of the Lord's Prayer, I put in "You know where I am; give the Sports Palast a good clout. It is being used as a place for talking over the air." Then I continued with the prayer.'

For the defence, Dr Reinhard H. Haferkorn, who was in charge of the English section of foreign broadcasts in Berlin, said that Ifan was introduced to him as a possible collaborator, but his scripts were not satisfactory, and that he was later employed on removing furniture from bombed-out flats. The professor stated that as far as his propaganda ministry was concerned, Ifan was a dead loss, but he was a very good furniture remover.

The findings and sentences of the Court Martial were promulgated, and the air-gunner I called Ifan, also known as Herr Becker and John Charles Baker, was convicted on charges of voluntarily aiding the enemy whilst a prisoner of war. He was sentenced to five years' penal servitude.

Embo, the Secretary, and Noel, the Choir-master, were Fighter Pilots, whereas the third member who was present at our mini-reunion, Bill Williams, was the Rear-Gunner on a Lancaster bomber. He had had a very unfriendly reception on the night of 25 October, 1944, when the Lancaster was shot down by heavy flak over Essen. He baled out and landed in a village called Kleve, and on reaching the ground he was attacked by hostile civilians who were actively encouraged and supported by a member of the Wehrmacht. He was beaten up and when he regained consciousness he discovered that he had been placed in the village Post Office, before being taken to a warehouse from which flour was distributed.

The next morning he was joined by a soldier from the Dorset Regiment who had been captured as a member of an advanced patrol in Holland, and who was suffering from severe head wounds. Both were taken from the warehouse to a local transit camp where they met two American pilots, an American Airborne soldier and a French Spitfire pilot. They had very little food at this centre, and very little sleep, as the straw palliasses attracted a number of unfriendly rats. Within a few days they were moved to another camp and joined a small group of Dutch Resistance fighters. Bill and the French Fighter Pilot attempted to escape but were detected by a guard who decided to spend the night with them. He was an authority on classical music and a Rear-Gunner and a French Pilot became his unwilling audience.

At dawn they were taken to the railway station at Brochalt, where they parted company, and Bill caught the Frankfurt train for Dulag Luft. He was placed in solitary confinement for four days, was questioned as to his political views, and was convinced that there was a determined effort to recruit prisoners to serve in the British Free Corps to fight against the Russians.

There were evocative Luft 7 smells. The first distinctive smell was that of the ever present pipe-smoking German guards who filled their pipes with the leaves of what was described by our hosts as 'mint tea', and which had a quite unique herbal aroma. This pale, yellow-green liquid was served every morning and had nothing to commend it except that it was hot and could be used as shaving water.

The second was the powerful smell of lime which was shovelled at night into the long pits which served as latrines, over which a thousand prisoners had previously balanced themselves precariously on a barbaric, primitive pole.

The third evocative smell was the result of German largesse, as very occasionally we received a ration of soft, watery cheese, which we squeezed out of a tube like brylcreem, and which stank to high heaven.

There were also familiar sounds which remain in the memory. The '*schnell, schnell, raus, raus*' of the guards outside; the constant 'tin-bashing' of inventive prisoners within the block;

and the sinister, but morale-boosting sound of the air-raid sirens.

We were not provided with eating or cooking facilities, and 'tin bashing', the conversion of empty tins from our Red Cross parcels by hammering them into pots, plates and frying pans, provided us with highly satisfactory utensils.

There were constant air-raid warnings, invariably about midday, when we regularly saw bombers of the American Air Force on their way to bomb the oil refineries in Rumania, and on two major raids on Breslau, only about sixty kilometres away. The order that all prisoners should remain in their huts during an air raid was strictly enforced. During one raid a Canadian Air Gunner, having heard the town 'all-clear', and thinking that it was the camp 'all-clear', walked out of his hut. He was shot by a German guard and died a few hours later.

The glorious summer weather continued until the end of October, but as winter approached the problems of keeping warm had to be tackled. Every hut contained a wood-burning stove, but the Germans did not consider it necessary to provide the wood, with the result that the reasonably well constructed wooden huts were stripped so severely of supporting timbers that it was a miracle that they had survived for so long. Our bed boards were sacrificed for the same purpose.

Our source of light were lamps made by melting cooking grease into small Red Cross tins, using a piece of cord or strands from clothes as wicks.

The contents of the parcels were used for many purposes, the most ingenious being the conversion of the large 'Klim' powdered milk tins into a highly efficient heating apparatus, known as the 'Blower'. This invention was often the only means available for bringing liquid to the boil, using little scraps of wood and paper for fuel.

The 'Blower' was too valuable an invention to be dismissed in a few words. There were many designs, some of them extremely intricate. The diagram overleaf was the type of blower used by Embo, and sketched by him many years later. The base was a piece of wood approximately 4 inches wide by eighteen

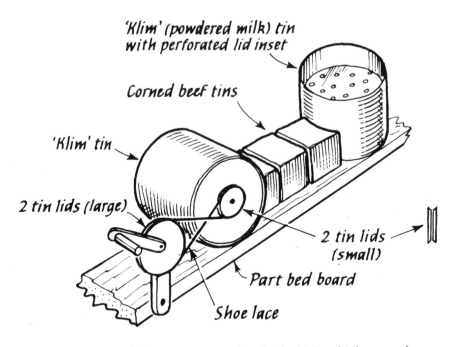

'Klim' (powdered milk) tin
with perforated lid inset

Corned beef tins

'Klim' tin

2 tin lids (large)

2 tin lids (small)

Part bed board

Shoe lace

inches long and three-quarters of an inch thick which was taken from someone's bed. The Klim and corned-beef tins provided us with vital additions to our diet on the rare occasions when we received Red Cross parcels, and the empty tins were now the essential components in this masterpiece of improvisation. The other parts were two large tin lids, two small tin lids, a perforated lid, a shoe lace and a large nail. A Klim tin and the corned-beef tins formed a tunnel, a handle turned a large wheel driving a smaller one at an increased pace and which turned a spindle which forced air through the corned-beef tunnel into the vertical Klim tin. This included a perforated piece of tin on which any small inflammable materials would be placed. This ingenious piece of equipment acted as a small forge and as well as boiling water, scraps of meat were heated in seconds.

There were three prisoners in our camp who were British Army captains – a Roman Catholic and a Church of England padre, and an Irish Medical Officer. The Irish doctor, Captain D. C. Howatson, performed miracles with inadequate resources in the first camp, and without any in the second. The Catholic priest looked after the spiritual well-being of those of his own faith and we saw very little of him in our compound. The Church of England padre, Canon John Collins, provided leadership of a very high quality to all our members irrespective of their religious beliefs, especially during the weeks of conflicting rumours, unease and uncertainty before the camp was eventually evacuated as a result of the advancing Russian armies. Our Padre's Sunday morning services were always well attended, and it was not by accident that the final hymn was always 'Glorious things of Thee are spoken, Zion city of our God' (*Molwn di, O Dduw ein tadau, Uchel wyl o foliant yw*) to the tune of Haydn's 'Austria'. As this was also the tune of '*Deutschland Deutschland Uber Alles*', the guards and the ferrets stood to attention, but could never understand why these airmen prisoners sang 'their' National Anthem. The singing of 'God Save the King' was forbidden, but our alternative 'Land of Hope and Glory' was accepted.

Ten years ago, on 20 March, 1982, I attended my first Stalag Luft 7 RAF Prisoner of War Reunion at the Polish Club in Nottingham, to thank the Guest of Honour, John Collins, this rather frail survivor who had given solid Christian leadership during the last three satanic months of the war in Europe. Six members of our little group were similarly motivated, so, in addition to Embo, Noel and Phil, another three met for the first time since the war to express their deep appreciation for his encouragement and example. Ted Sergeant, the camp comedian, had taken early retirement, Don Scopes, who, having experienced a few years of tight security in three camps, had become the Chief Security Officer at the National Museum of Wales, and Eric Raffill, who had graduated from being a flight engineer on a bomber to a senior engineer with the Post Office. The very articulate padre, who once gave our society a talk on his camping holiday in Switzerland in 1936, was overwhelmed by these tributes and was too emotional to respond.

My wife, Nesta, came with me to this reunion, and on the way out after an imaginative dinner with a menu based on the contents of a Red Cross parcel, she overheard one wife saying to another, 'You can always identify ex-prisoners of war as they never leave anything on their plate'.

To return to those last critical days in Stalag Luft 7, we were bombarded with conflicting rumours as to our future. We knew that the Russians were breaking through on the Eastern Front, and received daily reports on our concealed radio which was obtained as the result of bribery and blackmail. A friendly ferret on his daily hut inspection would be invited to share a cup of coffee and a piece of Red Cross chocolate. As this act of friendship was taking place, a prisoner would quietly steal his revolver and inform the poor man that unless he produced a radio or a component for a radio, he would be charged by his superiors for losing his weapon and would probably end up on the Eastern Front. He produced the radio.

Some of our members claimed that they received information from a much more reliable source as they were in tune with the spirit world. A ouija board was made in our barrack block from what remained of the wood from our bed-boards, with seances being held regularly in some of the huts. Soon after I arrived at Bankau, the self-styled prophet Nostradamus was taken much more seriously than the Allied or the German propagandists. It was said that Nostradamus had predicted that the war would end on 14 November, 1944, and the 'Spirits' were asked to confirm the date. I now realize that the participants in this desperate attempt at getting the truth always asked the spirits leading questions, such as 'Is the war going to finish on November 14th?' In our hut the answer always obligingly came up with 'Yes'. (One knock for 'yes', two knocks for 'no'.) There were tremendous arguments as to the value of these predictions, with supporters claiming that a prisoner in Hut 6 always got the right results.

On the expected day nothing happened and our war went on for another six months. There was a ceremonial burning of the ouija board. My colleagues, let down by the spirits, from then on relied on the BBC. It was not always good news and the report of the successful German Ardennes Offensive convinced us that Nostradamus had badly mis-calculated, and that it would probably be 1946 before we arrived home.

It was the news of the Russian winter offensive which restored morale and convinced us that we would be home long before the end of the war. At that time we never considered the possibility that the retreating Germans would take us with them.

We were told by our camp leader on 16 January, 1945, that the Russian armies were only eighty kilometres away, and on the 17th, at about eleven o'clock in the morning, we were given an hour in which to pack our kit and be ready to leave on foot. We were also informed by Oberfeldwebel Frank that for every man who fell out of the column on the march, five men would be shot. This threat was not carried out, but we were not unaware of the murder of fifty prisoners who had escaped from Stalag Luft 3 in Sagan in Lower Silesia.

After many false alarms we set out at 3.30 a.m on 19 January in a terrific blizzard on what was described by the English newspapers of the time as 'Prisoners' Worst Forced March in Germany – Survivors Too Weak To Talk'.

CHAPTER TEN

THE FORCED MARCH

This was never a 'march'. It was a head-down, rhythmic shuffle, by over a thousand prisoners for hundreds of miles from the frozen snow-covered wastes of Upper Silesia to an unknown destination in the general direction of Berlin, inadequately clothed, in sub-zero temperatures, and with hardly any food. When the march began, no transport was supplied for any sick who might fall out on the march, and the only medical equipment was carried on the back of Captain Howatson and three volunteers.

James Williams, who lived in my little corner of Dyfed, wrote in his autobiography, *Give Me Yesterday*: 'Time like a medieval Alembic distils the past, leaving memories to select what it wishes to remember; it is a catalogue of prejudices, of illogical likes and dislikes. We instinctively remember the past we wish to, discounting those which we do not.'

I find it difficult to write dispassionately of this grim experience, and was helped to get things into perspective by the photostat copies which we received at our Nottingham reunion of the Report which was sent to the Swiss Commission, acting as the Protecting Power. It was signed by the Camp Medical Officer, Captain Howatson, and Pilot Officer Peter Thomson, our Australian Camp Leader. It was dated 15 February, 1945, and gave a very objective account of the early stages of that dreadful experience, with details of the kilometres marched every day, of the evacuation of the sick, and of the number of kilogrammes of food issued by the German authorities. The 'Report of a Forced March Made by Occupants of Stalag Luft

7' underlined some of the problems and difficulties faced by 1,500 prisoners.

I also tried to get the reaction of one or two of my fellow prisoners, and the observation made by Bill Williams was very revealing and made one very significant point on our evacuation from Bankau: 'Most of us, Royal Air Force Aircrew, loaded ourselves with pots and pans, so that we looked like a travelling junk shop, but I noticed that the army Glider Pilot boys had only the minimum of kit. Realizing that they knew more about route marches than the Royal Air Force, I followed suit, and set off with only three blankets. I am unable to keep check of what happened on that march, but I know that I shall never forget it as long as I live. The conditions had to be seen to be believed and when we arrived at Stalag 3A morale was at its lowest point. Never did I think that I would welcome a prison camp, even though it was the oldest camp in Germany and an ex-concentration camp.' RAF aircrew had not been trained or prepared on the promenade in Blackpool or Brighton for the rigours of an Eastern European winter. But somehow we survived.

We left Bankau on 19 January and marched to Winterveldt, a distance of 28 kilometres. After an extremely cold march, we were eventually accommodated in small barns in what appeared to be a deserted farm. No food was provided. Next day we marched to Karlsruhe where we were housed in an abandoned brick factory, and for the first time an effort was made to give us food – two field kitchens to provide for the immediate needs of 1,500 men. Each field kitchen was actually capable of cooking sufficient food for 200 men. I was not at the receiving end of this largesse. There was a bonus for our dedicated Medical Officer, who was now provided with a horse and cart for the transport of the seriously sick. The cart was big enough to hold six sitting cases. After a rest period of eleven hours, we were ordered to move again, and the protests of the Camp Leader and the Medical Officer against further marching until we were adequately fed and rested were ignored. The German Abwehr Officer said that it was an order and must be obeyed. I would

have given anything to have remained at that hurriedly abandoned and still warm brick factory for a few more hours after
that long and bitterly cold night. We marched that night from
Karlsruhe to Schonfeld, where we arrived at 9 a.m on 21
January, a distance of 42 kilometres. The temperature was
minus 13 degrees centigrade. The Medical Officer's waggon was
filled after the first five kilometres, and from then on men were
being picked up at the roadside in a collapsed and frozen state.
A member of our group, Ken Hughes, had his frost-bitten toe
amputated without an anaesthetic by our gallant Medical
Officer.

After crossing the River Oder, a distance of 35 kilometres,
we were told that we would receive accommodation, and that
there would be no further move for two days. We huddled
together in the cowsheds and barns of a deserted farm and I had
the greatest difficulty the next morning in putting on my frozen
boots, as they were as stiff as wooden clogs, and were only
softened by burying them in a mixture of cow dung and straw.
There were ugly scenes the next morning as the Germans
ordered us to prepare to march immediately. It was 3 a.m and
very dark, and there was an inevitable delay as we could not
find our equipment. The guards became aggressive for the first
time, charged into our quarters with rifles firing above our
heads and at 5 a.m we were on the road again. By this time the
guards were becoming very frustrated on finding the number of
prisoners gradually decreasing after each stop-over, as they
could not account for twenty-three men who were missing.

On 24 January, after a march of 20 kilometres, we were
allowed to rest for most of the day in barns in Wanzen, where
a sick-bay had been been hurriedly prepared in a cowshed, and
thirty-one sick prisoners were evacuated to Sagan. It was in this
cowshed that Embo of Fagin fame lost his superiority, and in
considerable pain and great discomfort, he decided to approach
the Medical Officer to ask his advice how best to support this
embarrassing appendage. Within minutes he found himself on
his knees with a battered old bucket between his legs and
Captain Howatson holding a large syringe. Fagin was reduced

to normal size, as was the number of his friends, as without Fagin there would be no extended showers.

By 29 January many of our friends fell by the wayside, and the 22 kilometres between Standorf and Peterwitz, from 6 p.m in the evening until 4 a.m the following day, were covered in complete darkness, with a blizzard blowing the whole time. We were now utterly exhausted and were promised transport. This was not provided until we reached Goldberg on 5 February when we were put into cattle trucks, an average of 55 to 60 to each truck and left there for nearly four days.

Most of us were suffering from severe dysentery and the conditions inside these grossly overcrowded trucks, without enough space even to stretch our legs, leave nothing to the imagination. For four days, we had been lying in own own filth.

The Official Report to the Swiss Commission is a masterly understatement:

'February 5th. On arrival at Goldberg we were put into cattle trucks, an average of 55 men to each truck. By this time there were numerous cases of dysentery and facilities for men to attend to personal hygiene were inadequate. The majority had no water on the train journey for two days. When the men were allowed out of the trucks to relieve themselves, many of the guards ordered them back inside again and we had to be continually getting permission for the men to be allowed out. We were on the train from the morning of February 5th until the morning of February 8th.'

My parents had kept a copy of the *Daily Telegraph* of 11 April, 1945, which gave details of the camps which had been liberated and gave prominence to this forced march. The correspondent wrote: 'I have been talking to some of the survivors of the 6,000 British, American and Russian prisoners of war who took part in one of the worst forced marches of the war. Some of the men marched nearly 500 miles, some 300 miles. Though they were occasionally clubbed with rifles en route, men died mostly from exhaustion, malnutrition and dysentery. In most cases the men were packed into a barn in darkness at night, so that no proper distribution of food was possible. Indeed some of the men went all day without food. During the march many fell out by the roadside, despite clubbing and kicking, to pick up dirty swedes from the fields. Once they had no water at all for 24 hours. Today, even after a few days' rest and care by an American medical unit, the majority of released prisoners are still too weak to talk except with long pauses.'

These official reports and press comments are all very useful correctives as the imagination can not always be trusted.

It was a march of despair, full of suffering, hate, bitterness and mutual distrust. As the conditions deteriorated and hunger became a reality, one was forced to hide one's portion of bread, and on one occasion I witnessed a group of men, once disciplined, fighting like animals around a dump of frozen sugar beet. Diarrhoea was rife, with men squatting in all sorts of places, and once in the middle of the main street of a small town. In front of us a stream of wretched refugees trudged on foot, or rode in farm carts, with all their belongings piled high on old lorries, horse-drawn carts and perambulators. They were not prepared to wait for what they had been warned would be the atavistic vengeance of the conquering Russians. The towns and villages appeared to be deserted, and we received a mixed reception from those who remained. Sometimes a request for water would be greeted with yells of '*tereur flieger*', but on one occasion when a fellow prisoner was on the point of collapse, he was given a glass of hot milk. The memorials to the fallen in the First World War were constant reminders of the futility of it all.

I am now informed that in parts of this huge column the guards used their rifle butts to beat prisoners crawling around in muddy fields, grubbing for swedes, but we were lucky, and our attempts to scrounge swedes and sugar beet were overlooked and possibly encouraged. It was one way of staying alive.

The German guards were properly clothed, and were presumably well fed, but the young men were fighting on the Eastern and Western Fronts, and our guards had as much difficulty as their prisoners in adapting themselves to these wintry conditions. I saw one or two middle-aged guards dragging their rifles in the snow, and I am told that there was one occasion when a guard had his rifle carried for him by a much younger prisoner. Sub-zero temperatures did not differentiate between friend and foe.

It would have been fairly easy to escape from the column, especially at night, and the threat that five men would be shot for every man who fell out of the column was not taken too seriously after the first few days. I had one splendid opportunity. We had a few hours' rest after a disastrous march in Upper Silesia, and without any difficulty, or danger, I was able to break away and shuffle into a small house. It was occupied by a Polish woman and her son, and she expressed her sympathy in a very practical way. She gave me a bucketful of porridge, which I devoured in minutes. My intention was to stay there until our Russian allies liberated the area, and I was on the point of making myself understood when the door opened and a German officer walked in. He looked at me, and said firmly, and very politely, 'Will you please return to your comrades; you are making it very difficult for all of us'. I obeyed. Perhaps it was just as well, as the few who broke away on this march had the greatest difficulty in convincing the Russian officers that they were British prisoners of war and not deserters. The Russians had other things on their mind, such as capturing Berlin. The British prisoners who convinced them ended up in Odessa, the Black Sea port which was open to allied shipping, but the British Red Cross was called upon to provide them with food before they were eventually taken home.

There were a number of heroes on that march whose courage will never be acknowledged, such as the airmen who carried a fellow prisoner for nearly fifty miles over the barren and frozen wastes of Upper Silesia. One of our members has been belatedly acknowledged by his fellow prisoners, but not by his Government: The Reverend Canon John Collins, whose encouragement and example kept many of us marching on across Silesia when all we wanted to do was to sit down and freeze. His words were recalled at our Nottingham reunion: 'Only another four kilometres – we are stopping there'.

The authors of the official Report for the attention of the Swiss Commission wrote the following summary:

'As a result of this march and the deplorable conditions, the morale of the men is extremely low. They are suffering from an extreme degree of malnutrition, and at present, an outbreak of dysentery. There are numerous cases of frostbite and other minor ailments. They are quite unfit for any further movement. Food and better conditions are urgently required. We left Bankau with no Red Cross supplies and throughout the march all the rations were short issued, the most outstanding being bread, which amounts to 2,524 loaves.'

Only the fighter pilot with the deep scar and the spectacularly restored testicle could introduce an element of humour into this grim drama. He witnessed a guard who had found a bottle of Schnapps struggling across a distant field deep in snow, shouting at the top of his voice, 'Fuck Hitler'.

We arrived in Stalag 111A, Luckenwalde, on 9 February, 1945, and after four days cooped up in cattle trucks, we staggered erratically from the station to the camp, which was only two kilometres away. Our long march had ended, and so had Himmler's plans for the 'Greater Germania' which was to include Denmark, Norway, Belgium and the Netherlands.

Hitler was fully aware of the plight of the prisoners on that march and the following entry appears in the Goebbels Diaries:

'The Führer is violently opposed to any steps being taken to assist Anglo-American prisoners of war now in process of transfer from the East to the neighbourhood of Berlin. There are some 78,000 of them and they can no longer be properly fed; they are riddled with lice and many of them are suffering from dysentery. Under present circumstances there is little one can do for them. Perhaps it would be possible to call in the Red Cross to help in producing a semi-human existence for them.'

We had survived, but there was little to celebrate in that incubus of horror and utter despair during the dying months of a rapidly disintegrating Third Reich.

CHAPTER ELEVEN

STALAG 3A: LUCKENWALDE AND THE LONG LIBERATION

On 18 August, 1989, I attended a meeting of the Council of the National Museum of Wales in Cardiff. Sitting next to me was an old friend from my Pembrokeshire days, John Barrett, a former Warden of Dale Fort in that county. John served with the regular Air Force before the war, and when war was declared the young Squadron Leader pilot assumed that he would gain rapid promotion and would soon become at least a Group Captain. He was shot down on his first mission and that was the end of a promising career. Although we had worked together on many occasions, it was only a few months before the Council Meeting that we discovered that we had been on the same march from Poland and that we had both ended up in Luckenwalde, about forty miles south-west of Berlin. When I asked him, 'Do you remember Luckenwalde, my old friend?' he exploded and shattered the peace of the seriously minded Museum Council group by bellowing, 'Wasn't that a bloody awful place'. That sums it up.

We were now eye-witnesses to the war's most dramatic conflict, the Battle of Berlin – the Gotterdammerung of the Third Reich.

Stalag 3A, Luckenwalde, was not an RAF prisoner of war camp. Besides officers and men of the British Army, there were Americans, Russians, French, Italians, Czechs, Norwegians, Jugoslavs and Belgians – about 16,000 men in all. The Senior Allied Officer was General Ruge, a Norwegian. The conditions were deplorable and when a Russian Captain arrived to take over the administration of the camp he was horrified at the living conditions of the prisoners.

148

During the first month there were no Red Cross food parcels and, according to a report published after the war, the German rations did not amount to more than fifteen hundred calories a day. The whole camp was slowly starving. I was told at the time that the Red Cross parcels had been diverted to the French compound by the French prisoners who were allowed to work in the railway depot. For fuel, our bunk beds were broken up and used as firewood. As we were not allowed to leave the camp to work, we were in a more desperate situation than the other ranks who were allowed to work outside. If they were fortunate enough to be assigned to farms or factories, it was sometimes possible to scrounge food. I shall never forget the generosity of two Belgian Army prisoners who worked on the land during the day and occasionally brought me some potatoes. They were called Frans Broeckaert and Georges, and I promised Frans that I would get in touch with his wife should I arrive home before his release. She lived in Mechelin, and I was able to inform her that he was still alive and well. I received the following letter from him dated 10 July, 1945:

'My dear Jim,
I send you my best thanks for sending my letter from Luckenwalde to my wife. She was very pleased to receive it, also were my daughter and son. They all wish to thank you as well for sending the good news that I was coming home. I arrived home four weeks after you. I wish from my heart that you are all very well at home also your family, and the best of health and happiness. I think that these few words will please you, and I will remember our rendezvous in Belgium. I hope you will write to me a letter to say when you are coming. Many handshakes from me. Your friend, Frans Broeckaert.'

I tried to honour my promise to get in touch with Frans in Mechelin. It was All Saints' Day, and the police station was manned by a solitary officer who was not particularly pleased to be disturbed by a nostalgic Warrant Officer who wanted to find a former member of the Belgian Army. There were three Broeckaerts on the electoral register and I visited all three, but my Frans was not one of them. I wonder what happened to him, and I am very sorry that I was unable to thank him in person for those few potatoes.

I think I was helped to survive by my good Belgian friends, and in addition, I queued every morning outside the Serbians' barracks for their hot potato peelings. I was now very weak, and for the first time I experienced what real hunger meant. There were occasions when I would wake at night from a realistic dream to see a tin of condensed milk floating in the air. It was always a tin of condensed milk. I collapsed one morning, and can vaguely remember being carried by an Irish Guards Sergeant, Paddy Doyle, to a bunk in a hut which was reserved for the very sick. There were no medical supplies.

There were many Irish prisoners in Luckenwalde and I was told by Paddy that the Germans had brought them there from various prison camps in the hope that they could be persuaded to enlist in the British Free Corps and fight by the side of the Wehrmacht on the Russian front. The attempt was a complete failure.

The British Free Corps was the inspiration of John Amery, who tried to recruit British and Commonwealth POWs in German hands, with the promise of better food, better living conditions and, above all, the company of women. Ronald Seth in *Jackals of the Reich* states that between 900 and 1,200 Irishmen were collected from various prison camps and brought to Luckenwalde, and attempts to indoctrinate them were made by a Swiss Nazi, SS Captain Hans Lindt, the propaganda officer of the Luckenwalde commandant. Each man was issued with the following message: 'Soldiers of the British Commonwealth! Soldiers of the United States of America. The great Bolshevik offensive has now crossed the frontiers of Germany. The men in the Moscow Kremlin believe the way is open for their conquest of the Western world. This will certainly be the decisive battle for us. But it will also be the decisive battle for

England, for the United States and for the maintenance of Western civilization. Are you for the culture of the West or the Barbaric Asiatic East?' These loyal Irish soldiers did everything they could to accommodate us in their compound.

Although the conditions in the camp were deplorable, the news of the Russian advance, which was converging steadily on Berlin, helped to maintain morale. Most of the German guards were now convinced that the war was nearly over, though one or two still believed that Hitler would produce a secret weapon that would give them victory. They were scared of the Russians and hoped that the British and Americans would arrive first. One of them shook my hand and said, 'Before long we shall be fighting the Russians together.'

In the days before liberation there was continuous gunfire in the woods around the camp, together with aerial activity at night. It was on such a night that I witnessed for the first time a cold-blooded murder. There was an air-raid warning and a prisoner lit up a cigarette. Another prisoner, shrivelled by years of neglect and an untreated disease, shouted, 'Put that cigarette out, you bastard. I'll get you in the morning'. He must have been on the prowl all night, found an iron bar, and with the strength of a madman killed him. We were helpless and there was nothing we could do about it.

During the second week in April a contingent of RAF prisoners from our compound were marched to the station and told that they were to be transferred to Munich. Once again they were placed in the familiar 'Six horses, 40 men trucks', and, fully aware of the devastation which allied rocket-firing aircraft could inflict on trains, were allowed to paint POW on the roof. They waited nervously in the trucks for a day, but the engine which was to take them to their new camp failed to appear and on 14 April they returned. Prisoners and guards were now convinced that if the German army could not provide a railway engine the end must be very near.

There are two abiding memories of a visit I made one day with Ifan and Noel to the adjacent Russian compound. The Russian prisoners, derided as sub-human Slavs, brutalized and starved, had transformed a bare barrack block into a Church with impressive mosaics covering the eastern wall, where these sad, etiolated survivors were able to enjoy the moral freedom which accompanied an unquestionable faith. 'Window', the bundles of tinfoil dropped by thousands of bombers to cloud the enemy radar screens, had been used by these imaginative artists to open a window to eternity.

There were many deaths among the Russian prisoners, and at this time there was a strong possibility of an outbreak of typhus. The dying were largely ignored and the dead were placed in sacks and unceremoniously carted away in trucks.

The centre of activity in this RAF compound was not a Church but a toilet block. We were not unaccustomed to the debilitating effect of severe dysentery, but it had now assumed alarming proportions. There were long bedraggled crocodile queues to see our gallant doctor, who was powerless to help, as there were no medical supplies. He was, nevertheless, a good psychologist and suggested that we should toast the remains of the eighth, or later the twelfth, of our loaf into charcoal and eat it. We accepted his advice and, black-mouthed, survived in the filth and squalor of our billet.

There was plenty of activity in the air and on the ground. Mosquitos of RAF Bomber Command made regular visits to Berlin, and the RAF and the 8th American Air Force were much in evidence. A dramatic night raid on Potsdam lit up the compound. On the ground the Stalag was in the direct line between the advancing American and Russian forces, much too near to the mortar-gun battle between the rapidly advancing Russians and the embattled remains of a crack SS German division who had visited the camp only the day before.

We continued to receive the news from our concealed radio and knew that the Western Allies had crossed the Rhine, and that the Russians had reached the Elbe. Both armies were racing towards our 'Big City', Berlin, and the only question in our mind was, 'Who will be the first to arrive?' These were not military considerations. Our political leaders had drawn up the new political map of Europe. The British, Canadian and American troops would stop at the Elbe, leaving the Russians to take Berlin.

On 21 April we discovered that the guard towers were no longer manned, and that the Germans had marched off, with the exception of about half a dozen who had surrendered themselves to us, and had thrown their weapons into a nearby lake. The German Commandant had handed over the camp to the Senior Allied Officer, General Ruge. The Administration building had been left intact and we all received our prison record cards.

A few dates are still imprinted on the memory. On Sunday, 22 April, a German aircraft strafed the camp, and on the same evening the Mayor of Luckenwalde came in and offered to hand over the town to the prisoners. This request was refused by General Ruge. We were prepared for dramatic events and were not disappointed. In the early hours of the morning a Russian light armoured car drove into the camp and the occupants were mobbed. There was tremendous excitement, bordering on hysteria. We assumed that we would soon be going home. Several hours later Russian tanks and armoured cars roared into the camp and parked outside the barracks. We were told that the town of Luckenwalde had fallen, though fighting continued in the woods surrounding the camp until 2 May.

The Russian prisoners were immediately set free, given weapons and joined the battle. They were physically in very bad shape but appeared anxious to follow the tanks on the final assault on Berlin. The Russian tank commander sat on his tank and shouted, '*Alles*' (All of you) and could not understand how the British and Americans could remain in a camp which had been liberated when the war was not over and Berlin was still standing.

This was not our war.

The tanks drove off, followed by the Russian prisoners, badly clothed and ill-equipped, but shouting triumphantly '*Deutschland Kaput*'. They probably marched to their death.

A young Russian officer arrived on 26 April to take over the administration of a camp of over 16,000 men and was appalled by the conditions under which we were living. He immediately made arrangements for the British and the Americans to be moved to a luxurious former German officers' camp a few miles away and which was large enough to accommodate all the prisoners with the exception of the Poles and the Italians. The French prisoners who had already occupied the camp were driven out by a Russian woman who had a tommy gun, but the camp had to be abandoned as a stream of refugees, many of them armed, arrived, and had no intention of leaving. Even a gallant lady with an automatic weapon could not cope with this situation.

We were now free, but it was to be another six weeks of great tension and low morale before we were allowed to go home. General Ruge left the camp, and the Senior British Officer was put in charge of the internal administration. The population of the camp had now doubled, with the addition of two thousand Italian internees and an influx of refugees, so the food situation became even more desperate. There was a serious danger of epidemics and a Russian doctor, a young woman, inoculated the British and American prisoners against typhus. Water and electricity had been cut off. The Russians allowed parties of prisoners to go into the town to bring in as much food as they could and provided them with an armed escort. A certain amount of meat was brought in 'on the hoof' and a cow was slaughtered in the toilet block.

It was at this critical time of hunger, low morale and great uncertainty as to our future that I witnessed a spontaneous act of generosity and humanity. The Russian tank commander broke down the fences which segregated the various national groups, discovered the accumulation of Red Cross parcels which had been diverted into the French compound and released them to the 'Allies'. He said that there were only three allies – the Russians, British and Americans – and that they should be the only recipients. The Russians were on the road to Berlin and the British and Americans decided that these life-saving Red Cross parcels should be shared between all the other nationalities. It was the right decision, but hunger remained.

We had instructions from our Senior British Officer that no escape should be attempted and that no one should leave the camp until transport had been organized. Two members from the RAF compound had already lost their lives trying to break out over the wire and patience was essential. Nevertheless, many prisoners, including a number from our Welsh Club, began to leave the camp on their own in the hope of reaching the American zone, some on foot, some on stolen bicycles and one on horseback. Some got through, but most of them were picked up by the Russians and brought back to the camp.

On 6 May an American officer arrived with a convoy of lorries and stated that he had orders to evacuate Americans, British, Norwegians and French, in that order. In the middle of the operation Russian troops appeared and began to fire over the heads of the prisoners, ordering them out of the lorries. I was one of of the last to leave Luckenwalde and removed from the Notice Board the original letter from the Senior British Officer to the Russian authorities. It expresses the mood of despair and utter frustration which we all experienced. I reproduce this faded letter as it was written:

'The Senior British Officer is communicating the following in writing to the Russian authorities here today.

'FROM: Senior British Officer, Stalag 111A
To Russian Commandant for Repatriation, Stalag 111A.

May 7, 1945.
'In order to avoid misunderstanding, I am putting into writing the principal statements which I made at our conference last night.

'The situation of the British at this camp is now as follows. From the 22nd April I, at the request of the Russian Authorities, have been responsible for the administration and security of this entire camp of 18,000 mixed nationalities. The work of the camp during this time has been carried out mainly by British and American officers and men. It should, however, be appreciated that, owing to the Russian orders re confinement to camp etc, we have had to continue to all intents and purposes as prisoners. That these orders were a military necessity is of course clear, but nevertheless the result has been a lowering of the spirit of all ranks. It is important to understand and make allowances for the mental attitude of prisoners of war who have been liberated but are still denied their freedom.

'The food situation, up to yesterday, was precarious, and the daily ration, even though assisted by American supplies, is still grossly inadequate. It is realized that the Russian authorities overcame great difficulties in providing food at all under harassing circumstances; but it will also be agreed that the supply organization of this camp performed most of the work. Furthermore, the camp has become even more over-crowded owing to the influx of Italian refugees. The problems of sanitation are considerable, and the general health is threatened.

'In spite of all this, the Russian orders were obeyed and control was maintained up to the 5th of May. On that day an American officer, representing Supreme Allied Headquarters, arrived with instructions to evacuate the Americans and British in that order. His credentials were not accepted by the Russian authorities here, who stated that they could not allow such an evacuation to proceed since they had no orders on the subject. An ambulance convoy, which also arrived on this day, was permitted to evacuate all Americans and a few British sick.

'Yesterday the American representative from Supreme Allied Headquarters returned with a convoy to carry out his orders. Capt Tchekanov, acting as deputy for Capt Medvedev, who was sick, refused to allow him to proceed with his duties. Later, when an attempt was made to proceed with the evacuation, armed force was used against American troops to prevent their leaving the camp.

'No doubt this whole affair is due to misunderstanding, but the situation created is extremely serious. In spite of continual assurances that we were to be repatriated with the least possible delay, we now see the Russians actively preventing such repatriation. It is impossible for me to explain or justify such action in the eyes of my officers and men. I warned Capt Medvedev on the 4th May that such a situation was likely to arise, and that, if it did, I could not be responsible for the consequences.

'Last night I was informed, for the first time, that the chief obstacle to our repatriation was that the registration was not complete. I have repeatedly offered to undertake the whole task of registration. I could have completed it by now if my offer had been accepted. In any case, I cannot believe that the Russians intend that vital interests should be threatened for the sake of mere formality.

'As the Senior British Officer here I am responsible, above all else, for the welfare of my officers and men. This welfare is seriously endangered by the present situation. I therefore demand that the position may be clarified without delay, and that our repatriation may be proceeded with immediately. Failing this, I must ask to be enabled to communicate with my Government.

'Finally I must point out that the present situation renders my position as Senior Allied Officer untenable. I therefore resign that position and from now on must be regarded as responsible only for the British.'

We were now convinced that there were political motives behind the refusal of the Russians to evacuate us. My good friend Embo was boiling a can of water on his home-made 'Blower' when I greeted him with the words, 'Well, Embo bach, you may still see Siberia'. He hit me hard. You did not joke about that possibility. It was not to be ruled out. We were prisoners of the Russians.

We were right in our suspicions that there were political considerations and, in his Report, Aidan Crawley wrote:

'The spirit of the prisoners sank, and they began to suspect political motives. This seemed to be confirmed a day or two later when the Russians broadcast that the Allies were with-holding 800 Russian officers who had been captured fighting with the Germans in Normandy shortly after D-Day. The men began to wonder whether they were to become pawns in an Allied struggle and were to remain in captivity indefinitely.'

We were told on 7 May that all German forces had surrendered unconditionally and on 8 May, 1945, VE Day was declared – 'Victory in Europe'. Our victory could not be celebrated for another two weeks – twenty-nine days after our release by the Russian Army, when a Russian Colonel announced that the remaining 2,000 British and eighty American prisoners would be taken to the Elbe in a convoy of Russian lorries.

On 20 May we left Luckenwalde in American trucks, but with Russian drivers. As I climbed into a truck outside the camp, I saw an elderly German civilian in a well-cut and expensive looking suit, waist-coat, collar and tie, lying on his back, with a revolver by his side. His dream of a triumphant Third Reich had been shattered and he could not face the consequences.

Within the barbed wire, we had heard the sound of battle, and now on our horrendous freedom journey through the woods south of Berlin, on unmade roads and avoiding bridges which had been destroyed, we saw all the evidence of the ravages of total war. There were the charred bodies of men still left hanging on dead trees. Everywhere there was death and decay. We eventually reached the banks of the River Elbe and, as we walked across the hastily constructed pontoon bridge, we passed a long queue of Russian ex-prisoners of war marching in the opposite direction. Fair swop.

On the other side of the pontoon, symbolic of the 'Great divide' which heralded the Cold War, a fleet of American trucks, with American drivers, carried us in reasonable comfort over bridges which had already been repaired to the American base at Halle Leipzig, which we reached in the late afternoon. I had at last reached Leipzig, the original target of Lancaster K-King, but it had been a long, devious and unexpected route.

There are vivid memories of our American reception, and on the rare occasions when a few of us meet as former prisoners of war, there are two abiding memories – the whiter than white bread which replaced the German ersatz black bread, and proper soap. We could not take advantage of the superb food given to us by our generous American hosts, as our digestive systems had not come to terms with the rapid transition from a twelfth of a loaf of black bread, half a cup of '*Kohlrube*' (coal turnip) soup and a few small potatoes, for what was regarded as a normal meal for the American forces. We were soon flown out in the trusty American Dakota DC3 aircraft to Brussels, and sitting next to me were two former Luft 7 prisoners, Leslie Woodward, the Australian Navigator whom I had first met in Antwerp prison, and Ifan, the man we suspected of collaboration. As the plane landed the RAF Military Police were there to receive Ifan.

We were taken to a brilliantly organized Canadian transit camp, where arrangements were made for our final repatriation. We entered one end of the system as scruffy, dirty, unkempt individuals who had been in the same clothes since we left Dulag Luft, and arrived at the other end, having been cleaned, identified, documented, deloused and kitted out with new clean clothes. We were given the freedom of a city in which I had previously been a civilian prisoner. An RAF Welfare Officer gave us five pounds each and said, 'Have a good time, boys'. We were too confused and too weak to do anything about it.

After a night of freedom in the Belgian capital, we left early next morning on a short flak-free flight in 'the fastest heavy bomber in the world' – a Lancaster. It touched down on an airfield somewhere near Oxford, and a reception party of ATS army women lined the runway.

Aidan Crawley concluded his official report on Luckenwalde with these words: 'So ended captivity. There can be few who would willingly live through it again, but there must be many who still draw inspiration from the knowledge that much can be endured and that to those who have once lost it, freedom has a value which is worth all the sacrifices which have been made for it.'

But in the words of John Barratt: 'It was a bloody awful place'.

There was an emotional reception two days later when I arrived home. The entire village turned out for the official welcome to the only member of that closely knit community who had been once declared 'Missing, presumed killed' and who had returned. My parents and my brother, Nefydd, were in the hired car which was driven by Griff-y Bys from Carmarthen station to my local village. It was towed in for the last few hundred yards by my former school friends and 'Mishtir', the village schoolmaster, who, on behalf of the welcoming committee, read welcome-home messages which included a telegram from the Resistance Courier, Tiny Mulder.

The annual *Cymanfa Ganu* (Singing Festival) took place in Cilfowyr Chapel on the following Sunday, when the conductor, Andrew Williams, asked the congregation to sing 'Cwm Rhondda' as he had been told that it was the signature tune of the Luft 7 Welsh Society.

As a result of severe malnutrition during the last few months of the war, and the rigorous march from Poland, I was now under six stone in weight and suffered from muscular rheumatism. After a few weeks of being thoroughly spoilt at home, I was sent to the RAF hospital in Cosford, where I received first class medical attention, which included physiotherapy and heat treatment. The daytime benefits were unfortunately often cancelled out by the overwhelming generosity of the local inhabitants in the evenings.

There is one experience which I find very difficult to convey in words – the consciousness of strength and health rushing through, and re-entering my body.

The month in the hospital in Cosford was followed by another month in a Rehabilitation Centre in Sunningdale Park in Berkshire, where we were instructed by well-meaning civilians on how to adapt ourselves to peacetime Britain. (I remember one pompous industrialist opening his remarks by saying that he was a well-known Yorkshire flannel merchant, and could not understand why his well intentioned words were greeted with howls of laughter: 'flannel merchant' had quite a different meaning for most of us.) It did not take us long before we were well and truly rehabilitated. The impressive stone lions at the entrance to this historic home disappeared one evening: the former prisoners of war had come to terms with post-war Britain.

I was discharged from the Royal Air Force on health grounds, but before exchanging my newly acquired Warrant Officer uniform (aircrew promotion was more or less automatic up to a certain rank), for the Government demobilization suit – a navy blue pinstriped double-breasted suit, a felt hat, black shoes, shirt and an Air Force tie – there was one final assignment. It was to represent the Royal Air Force on a 'Goodwill Mission' to meet members of the Resistance in Holland and Belgium and to thank them on behalf of the Service for the help which they had given to the airmen who had been shot down over their country.

My first call was to the house from which I had been betrayed, 79 Isabellalei, in Antwerp. The Staquet family were still alive, and I was greeted by Fernand with the words – 'Monsieur, I have for you your pipe'. My Oosterwolde pipe had also survived.

During the next week I visited all my contacts in the Resistance and my previous hosts in the Netherlands. I had every reason to thank them.

Never was there a mission so willingly carried out.

POSTSCRIPT

There has been a continuous association over many years with most of the people who appear in this Memoir, but with one notable exception, K-King's Bomb Aimer, Ronald Aitken. As I have failed to contact him, he does not appear in this narrative, though his experiences were very similar to mine, when, after a period 'Underground', he was captured and imprisoned.

I often wondered what had become of the American pilot, Valleau Wilkie, after he left the remote Frisian farm on the escape route to the south. Nearly fifty years later, on 7 June, 1993, on a ferry from Holyhead to Dublin, I sat next to an American lady, Janet Tyson, and when I said that I'd been recently trying to contact a Valleau Wilkie in New Jersey, she said, 'I know a Valleau Wilkie'. As a result of this chance encounter, I received a letter from Fort Worth in Texas, with the following opening sentence 'It seems quite incredible – Yes, I am the Valleau Wilkie you knew in Friesland, long, long ago. In accordance with Underground practices, I did not know the names of the people who helped me, though I have vivid memories of events'.

To Wilkie, 'it seems quite incredible,' but to our Welsh poet, Dylan Thomas, 'the only surprising thing about miracles, however small, is that the sometimes happen.'

Of my hosts in the Netherlands and in Belgium, six are now at rest: Pieter and Hinke Dijkstra, Lambert Tiesinga, Simon de Cock and Fernand and Mme Staquet. My last words to them in 1944 were: 'You must come to stay with us in Wales as soon as the war is over'. They accepted my invitation, but unfortunately they nearly all decided to come at the same time in the summer of 1946: Pieter and Hinke Dijkstra and young Elisabeth, Simon and Dina de Cock, Ruurd and Alie Postma on their honeymoon, and Tiny Mulder's brother who was stationed with the Dutch Army in England. A Protestant worker in a milk factory in Friesland and a Catholic industrialist from Brabant mixed freely, united by their complete loyalty to the cause for the liberation of their country and by their contribution in that heroic struggle.

This was a new and memorable experience for the Dijkstra family who were travelling for the first time in a train, and not by cycle, and to a foreign country. I met them in London and a day of sightseeing nearly ended in disaster. Exhausted, we finally arrived at the Albert Memorial, where Hinke made a dramatic statement which nearly ruined their great expectations for the holiday of a lifetime: '*Ach, Ik heb myn zak verloren*' (I have lost my bag). Peter advanced a few steps up the Memorial and pronounced in a loud voice: '*Een nooie dag, maur een verschrikkelijke avond*' (a nice day but a terrible evening): we had to find the bag, which contained a £5 note and two silver tie-pins, one for me and one for my brother. I revisited all the places of interest, but our search was of no avail. Pieter became very dejected, but I was able to convince him in the end that the British police would do everything possible to find the bag. Two days later in Boncath, PC Gronow came on his bicycle with the bag, with the £5 note, and the silver souvenirs. The holiday had been saved, and to celebrate this outstanding example of the efficiency of the police force and the honesty of the British people, my father hired a mini-bus to take our guests to Tenby. It rained all day.

A few months later my mother and I visited the Dijkstra family, and all our other Dutch friends, and a few years later the same itinerary was carried out, but this time it was on our honeymoon, when I was able to introduce my wife, Nesta, to the families which she had heard so much about.

Years later, my wife and I and our two daughters, Sian and Rhian, went to see Pieter in hospital in Leeuwarden. He organized the hospital staff as he had organized us all in his little home in Garijp. Within minutes of our arrival at his sick bed, the Matron arrived with an iced cake bearing the words '*Hartelijk welkom*', followed by an obedient nursing Sister carrying a tray with generous helpings of ice-cream and orange juice for our greatly impressed young daughters. Pieter was still 'the boss'.

Hinke died in 1957, aged 60, and Pieter in 1970 after a long illness, at the age of 68.

My next visit to Friesland was in 1972, when I tried unsuccessfully to find Pieter's grave in Garijp. There was a simple explanation, as Pieter had told his nephew, Ruurd, 'There will be no gravestone and no nonsense. When I go, I go'. This was typical of this stubbornly independent man. He was never the type to go 'gently into that good night'.

In 1991 Elisabeth compromised by placing a simple cross on the graves of her parents, so that her children could be made aware of their last resting place.

Lambert Tiesinga was very ill when we visited him in 1985, and had to remain in a room which had to be kept at a certain temperature. Nevertheless he insisted on having his photograph taken with us; he was dressed in his best suit, and wore his Resistance Medal. I thought it was in my honour, but no, it was the Queen's Birthday. He had retired from his farm, Romsicht, and he and his caring wife had moved to a smaller house in the town.

Vrouw Tiesinga and her daughter Tiny, who was a baby when we first met, came to stay with us three years ago, and the good vrouw came on her own a year later.

The association with Simon and Dina de Cock and their family was a continuous one with frequent visits in Holland and Wales. I was regarded as one of the family and had the immense pleasure of being present at significant family gatherings such as the wedding of two of their children, Wim and Mieke. The last time I saw my old friend, Simon, was on 10 June, 1989, when I took part in a series of Welsh language television programmes on the Second World War – 'Amser Rhyfel' (War Time). I was filmed in the very cell which I once occupied in Antwerp jail and the next day I introduced the television team to some members of the wartime Resistance in Belgium and Holland. Lucy, Fernand Staquet's daughter, was interviewed in their old home in Isabellalei, and the de Cock family in Tilburg. The television crew were well received by

Simon and Dina, and their daughter Mieke was the hostess. Simon was now in constant pain and confined to a wheelchair. In addition to his acute physical problems he was suffering from bouts of depression, and was constantly questioning the part which he played during the Occupation. He had been criticized by some for risking the lives of his wife and young family by his Resistance activities. It was only after a great deal of persuasion by Dina and Mieke that he agreed to take part in the programme, and only on the clear understanding that the film would not be shown on Dutch television. The producer, Selwyn Roderick, agreed and the interview took place. The man who had emigrated to New Zealand at the age of eighty had come home to his native Brabant, and in a quiet voice, suffused with an ineffable weariness, he ended his interview with these memorable words, 'We are living in difficult times but we must have absolute faith in the Almighty and Mrs Thatcher.'

I had the opportunity to mention this to the Prime Minister a few days later when she attended a Meeting of the National Society for the Prevention of Cruelty to Children in London. As a result, the Prime Minister wrote a letter reproduced here to thank him for his contribution to the Allied Cause fifty years ago.

Simon died two months later and on 13 August, 1989, I attended his funeral in Tilburg. A memorial pamphlet which included his picture was distributed at the Requiem Mass. He was wearing the Wartime Resistance Cross and a tie which I immediately recognized, as I had given it to him on one of his visits. It was the tie of the Beaumaris Baron Hill Golf Club. Halfway through the Priest's tribute, Dina jumped up and shouted, *'Dank U, Dank U'*. We all shared in this spontaneous tribute, and at least thirteen former airmen would have every reason to echo these words. Thank you, Thank you.

Mr and Mrs Staquet always received us with warmth and generosity and, though they were unable to visit us in Wales, we had the pleasure of welcoming their daughter Lucy and her husband Georges. Lucy wrote to tell me that her grandson had been named Jim 'in memory of you'. I wished him well in spite of this handicap.

1O DOWNING STREET
LONDON SW1A 2AA

THE PRIME MINISTER   8 May 1989

Dear Mr. de Cock

Dr. Davies has written to me to draw my attention to the help which you gave to him in May 1944 when, during the German occupation, at great risk to your family and yourself, you hid him in your home after his aircraft had been shot down in Holland.

I understand that Dr. Davies was not the first or only allied airman to be helped by you in this way and that by the end of the war you had given assistance to no less than eight others.

I know that throughout the Second World War it was the source of comfort and reassurance to our airmen to know that, if misfortune overtook them while flying over the occupied countries, there were people such as yourself who would help them on the ground even though the danger in doing so was so great.

I can but express my admiration for you for what you did in this way in the fight for freedom and the allied cause in those perilous days more than 40 years' ago. We in Britain have much to thank you for.

Yours sincerely

Margaret Thatcher

Mr. S. de Cock

166

Of my former hosts, two are indestructible and have survived in spite of wartime tensions and peacetime concern and worry for their husbands during long periods of severe illness and depression. Both these proud and independent ladies now live alone, Mrs Tiesinga in Oosterwolde, and Mrs de Cock in Tilburg. An occasional phone call and frequent visits keep a friendship of nearly fifty years very much alive.

The main link with the de Cock family is the little girl who once said, 'I met a man in the bath with big eyes,' the beautiful and loyal daughter, Mieke, whose new home near Antwerp is an extension of her own creative and artistic personality.

Jaap Boorsma and Piet Felix have retired after successful business careers, and Tiny continues to write creatively in the Frisian language.

On Thursday, 25 June, 1992, I spent a few nostalgic days with my old friend, Jaap Boorsma, in his new home in Dam-woude in Friesland. I willingly accepted his invitation to have lunch at the Hotel Princenhof in Eernewoude. There had been a major extension to the intimate thatched-roofed hotel we knew in 1944, the centre of the Resistance when we first visited the area. It was now just another hotel in a commercial chain, but the memory of the previous owner and resistance hero, Piet Miedema, had not been forgotten, as the avenue leading to the hotel had been named after him, and his youngest daughter was the owner of the lucrative sailing and tourist enterprise based on the tranquil and picturesque Lake Princenhoff. Piet gave us scarce food rations when we hid on Jaap's boat, risked his life on many occasions during the war, but was tragically killed a few days after his country had been liberated.

It was all so very peaceful on this placid lake, but in spite of our desperate attempt to pretend that we were men of the new Europe and living in the 1990s, we were both still in the Princenhoff of 1944.

In a *Guide to Friesland*, the area was described as an El Dorado for lovers of water sports and nature. It was also an El Dorado for escapers.

After a very good lunch, we travelled to Tolbert in the neighbouring province of Groningen to visit the graves of our Skipper, Jack Laurens, and the Rear Gunner, Don Bolt. Not only had these two graves been immaculately preserved, but bulbs had recently been planted and were in full bloom. When we asked who was responsible for this act, we were directed to the home of Herr Jo Weges, the retired headmaster of the local school, and were given an ecstatic welcome. Over countless cups of coffee and rich cream cake I happened to mention that, although I had kept in touch with all the people who had helped me in the Netherlands from the time when I arrived in Oosterwolde, I had no clear recall of the events during the first few days after landing, and did not know the names of the people, or my exact location.

My new contact, Mr Weges, phoned Jaap two days later to invite us to join him for coffee on the Sunday morning, and we arrived to be greeted by a houseful of people, a newspaper reporter and a photographer. Jo Weges had organized a brilliantly co-ordinated operation and had traced all the principal characters who were involved in the dramatic events on another Sunday morning long ago. It was a very emotional experience. The young girl who had called me a 'poor English Tommy', Betsy de Jong, now Betsy Visser-de-Jong and in her early seventies, presented me with the silk escape map which I gave her when I was hidden by her father, and on which I had marked the spot where we crashed. I was then introduced to Andries van der Donk whose farm was only a few hundred yards from where the plane had crashed and miraculously missed his house. He presented me with a piece of my parachute harness. Another guest was Weijer Veen from Marum, the son of the farmer who was prepared to help me when his neighbour took the easy way out by taking me to his farm and, with great relief, went home. Weijer said that my RAF uniform had been exchanged for his black trousers and a blue smock and that he wore my aircrew trousers for many years. He was the eldest of three children and a cousin to Betsy. It was his uncle, Jan Veen, who brought me by bicycle to the home of her father in Siegerswoude.

After numerous introductions, we were taken on a conducted tour in a series of cars to places which played a significant part in those first few days when I may have caused them certain problems and anxieties.

The first visit was to Andries van der Donk's farm, where he showed us the exact spot where K-King had finally crashed, and where he discovered two bodies, one of which was mutilated beyond recognition. The next was to the former home of Weijer Veen, and to the spot where I had landed and had hidden my parachute, about two miles from the wreckage. We then travelled through narrow lanes to a remote farm in Zevenhuisen where I was hidden for a day or two with Gerrit Wijkstra and his mother. When we arrived there on this nostalgic exercise, he was living on his own in this isolated and dilapidated farmstead, and was slightly disappointed when I did not immediately recognize him. I had no recollection of those few days, but at last I had the opportunity to thank him.

There was one other visit that afternoon in the Tolbert district which was the result of Jo Weges' detective work. He had discovered the resting place of our Wireless Operator, Cass Waight, who was buried in the cemetery in the neighbouring parish of Noordwyk. A War Graves Commission plaque was prominently displayed on the cemetery wall. As the church was about four miles away from Tolbert, where the plane landed, he must have been blown out of the plane – without a parachute.

I now know for the very first time of the events of those first few days before my contact with the Resistance and my arrival in Oosterwolde, the names of the people who helped me during a period of acute danger, and the approximate distance covered by foot and by cycle. All this activity took place within an area of not more than 50 kilometres.

On our return to Damwoude we visited my very first courier, Tiny Mulder, in Jellum, near Leeuwarden. Tiny was now the author of twenty books, including two novels, one book of short stories, numerous translations, and seven books of poetry. She recalled the hopes and idealism of the early post-war years, and was deeply disturbed by the resurgence of neo-Nazism and racisim in the Europe of the 1990s.

Tiny presented me with her recent book of poems in the

Frisian language, her poem 'May' reflecting her unease and ending with a warning. It must not be allowed to happen again.

'May'
Once – May 1945 –
when we danced like mad
in the squares
"don't fence me in"
freedom cried out
halleluja.

Then, there, we heard
what is called
the Voice of Freedom.
After that everything
returned to normal.
Come, let's go on;
no May since as yet has been
the right one.

Let's go
warn the children

There was a brief halt in Dokkum, the former home town of Jaap and Ruurd, where they first became involved in the Resistance struggle. We paused before a monument which stood on the spot where about twenty people were taken at random from the prison and were shot as reprisals for an attack by the Resistance on a German lorry carrying Dutch prisoners.

The inscription on this Resistance Memorial is a verse from Psalm 126:

1939–1945

Dy't mei triennen siedzje sille sjongend sichtsje

'They that sow in tears shall reap in joy'.